D1717898

AIRLINE INDUSTRY MERGERS: BACKGROUND AND ISSUES

Transportation Infrastructure - Roads, Highways, Bridges, Airports and Mass Transit

Additional books in this series can be found on Nova's website under the Series tab.

Additional E-books in this series can be found on Nova's website under the E-books tab.

TRANSPORTATION INFRASTRUCTURE - ROADS, HIGHWAYS, BRIDGES, AIRPORTS AND MASS TRANSIT

AIRLINE INDUSTRY MERGERS: BACKGROUND AND ISSUES

FELIX J. MERCADO
EDITOR

Nova Science Publishers, Inc.
New York

NOTICE TO THE READER

The Publisher has taken reasonable care in the preparation of this book, but makes no expressed or implied warranty of any kind and assumes no responsibility for any errors or omissions. No liability is assumed for incidental or consequential damages in connection with or arising out of information contained in this book. The Publisher shall not be liable for any special, consequential, or exemplary damages resulting, in whole or in part, from the readers' use of, or reliance upon, this material. Any parts of this book based on government reports are so indicated and copyright is claimed for those parts to the extent applicable to compilations of such works.

Independent verification should be sought for any data, advice or recommendations contained in this book. In addition, no responsibility is assumed by the publisher for any injury and/or damage to persons or property arising from any methods, products, instructions, ideas or otherwise contained in this publication.

This publication is designed to provide accurate and authoritative information with regard to the subject matter covered herein. It is sold with the clear understanding that the Publisher is not engaged in rendering legal or any other professional services. If legal or any other expert assistance is required, the services of a competent person should be sought. FROM A DECLARATION OF PARTICIPANTS JOINTLY ADOPTED BY A COMMITTEE OF THE AMERICAN BAR ASSOCIATION AND A COMMITTEE OF PUBLISHERS.

Additional color graphics may be available in the e-book version of this book.

LIBRARY OF CONGRESS CATALOGING-IN-PUBLICATION DATA

Airline industry mergers : background and issues / editor, Felix J. Mercado.
p. cm.
Includes index.
ISBN 978-1-61761-993-9 (hardcover)
1. Airlines. 2. Consolidation and merger of corporations. I. Mercado, Felix J.
HD9711.A2A37 2010
387.7'1--dc22
2010041278

Published by Nova Science Publishers, Inc. † New York

CONTENTS

PREFACE

Airline mergers do not always go as planned and/or realize their stated goals. The stockholders, employees, customers, and served communities often have competing interests in the merger process. Some stakeholders may support a merger at the outset of discussions, but change their mind over time. This book explores the impacts and issues of a United-Continental merger from a congressional perspective. Several major issues associated with the merger are discussed, including its potential effect on airfares, its effect on routes and services, whether employment is likely to increase or decrease, whether existing United-Continental airport hubs will retain their status in the future, how the United-Continental merger will affect further consolidation in the U.S. airline industry, and whether the merger will have a significant impact on industry profitability.

Chapter 1- The announcement that United Airlines and Continental Airlines would seek authority from the Department of Justice (DOJ) to merge would seem to indicate that consolidation continues in the airline industry. The announcement was well received by many within the aviation industry community. This is especially the case within the financial community, where there seems to be considerable support for industry consolidation. Nonetheless, there has been opposition to the merger in some quarters. Some consumer advocates are questioning the need for the merger, and some Members of Congress, notably House Committee on Transportation and Infrastructure (T&I) Chairman James Oberstar, have spoken out against its approval. Other interests, such as organized labor, are also wary of the merger and seek additional details about the specifics before they will support it.

Chapter 2- Earlier this month, United Air Lines (United) and Continental Airlines (Continental) announced plans to merge the two airlines and signed a merger agreement. This follows the acquisition of Northwest Airlines by Delta Air Lines (Delta) in 2008, which propelled Delta to become the largest airline in the United States. This latest merger, if not challenged by the Department of Justice (DOJ), would surpass Delta's merger in scope to create the largest passenger airline in terms of capacity in the United States. The passenger airline industry has struggled financially over the last decade, and these two airlines believe a merger will strengthen them. However, as with any proposed merger of this magnitude, this one will be carefully examined by DOJ to determine if its potential benefits for consumers outweigh the potential negative effects.

Chapter 3- I appreciate the opportunity to appear before you to discuss the current and future state of the airline industry and the role of the Department of Transportation (DOT) in the industry's ongoing restructuring. This hearing isin response to the proposed

United/Continentalmerger, a potential combination that has understandably captured the interest of this Committee and the American people.

Chapter 4 - Thank you for the opportunity to discuss the benefits and answer any questions related to the planned merger of equals between Continental Airlines and United Airlines that we announced on May 3. As we said at the time, this transaction will enable us to provide enhanced long-term career prospects for our more than 87,000 employees and superior service to our customers, especially those in small communities throughout the United States. Our combined company will be well-positioned to succeed in an increasingly competitive global and domestic aviation industry   better positioned than either airline would be standing alone or as alliance partners.

Chapter 5- The Machinists Union represents United Airlines and/or Continental Airlines workers in the flight attendant; ramp; customer service; reservation agent; fleet technical instructor; maintenance instructor; security guard; and food service employee classifications, plus customer service agents at United's frequent-flier subsidiary, Mileage Plus, Inc. The IAM also represents flight attendants at Continental's wholly-owned subsidiary Continental Micronesia and flight attendants at Continental and United regional partner ExpressJet Airlines. In total, the IAM represents more than 26,000 workers who will be affected by this proposed merger. Our bargaining relationship with each airline spans many decades.

Chapter 6- My testimony today focuses on the effects of the merger of United Airlines and Continental Airlines. I will also address the ongoing effects of consolidation in the airline industry that has been taking place for more than a decade. I am not speaking only for leisure travelers who make up more than 80 percent of airline passengers, but also for business travelers who provide more than 50 percent[1] of airline revenues.

Though these two airlines have many cooperative agreements, they still compete aggressively with each other in many ways — for corporate and leisure travelers, airline gates, frequent fliers, suppliers, travel agency attention and more.

Chapter 7- As background, I have been helping investors analyze the airline industry for 10 years and my firm does not seek investment banking business from the airlines.

As has been widely reported and recognized, the US airline industry, with the exception of low cost carriers, has been a financial failure. We've successive decades. And if there is one that fact that the industry is structured one, and there are a number of reasons for why this ahead.

Chapter 8- The U.S. passenger airline industry is vital to the U.S. economy. Airlines directly generate billions of dollars in revenues each year and catalyze economic growth. Interest in the airlines' ability to weather volatile fuel prices and the economic recession led to congressional requests for a GAO review. GAO examined how (1) the financial condition of the U.S. passenger airline industry has changed, the principal factors affecting its condition, and its prospects for 2009; (2) airlines have responded to the factors affecting their financial condition; and (3) changes in the industry have affected airports, passengers, and the Airport and Airway Trust Fund (Trust Fund), which funds the Federal Aviation Administration's (FAA) capital programs and most of its operations. To do this, GAO analyzed financial and operating data, reviewed studies, and interviewed airline, airport, and FAA officials and other experts. The Department of Transportation (DOT) provided technical comments, which were incorporated as appropriate.

Chapter 9- The airline industry is vital to the U.S. economy, generating operating revenues of nearly $172 billion in 2007, amounting to over 1 percent of the U.S. gross domestic product. It serves as an important engine for economic growth and a critical link in the nation's transportation infrastructure, carrying more than 700 million passengers in 2007. Airline deregulation in 1978, led, at least in part, to increasingly volatile airline profitability, resulting in periods of significant losses and bankruptcies. In response, some airlines have proposed or are considering merging with or acquiring another airline.

ISBN: 978-1-61761-993-9
© 2011 Nova Science Publishers, Inc.

Chapter 1

AIRLINE INDUSTRY MERGERS: ISSUES OF CONGRESSIONAL INTEREST

John W. Fishcer and Michaela D. Platzer

SUMMARY

The announcement that United Airlines and Continental Airlines would seek authority from the Department of Justice (DOJ) to merge would seem to indicate that consolidation continues in the airline industry. The announcement was well received by many within the aviation industry community. This is especially the case within the financial community, where there seems to be considerable support for industry consolidation. Nonetheless, there has been opposition to the merger in some quarters. Some consumer advocates are questioning the need for the merger, and some Members of Congress, notably House Committee on Transportation and Infrastructure (T&I) Chairman James Oberstar, have spoken out against its approval. Other interests, such as organized labor, are also wary of the merger and seek additional details about the specifics before they will support it.

Airline mergers do not always go as planned and/or realize their stated goals. The stockholders, employees, customers, and served communities often have competing interests in the merger process. Some stakeholders may support a merger at the outset of discussions, but change their mind over time, and the reverse, of course, is also true. This chapter briefly looks at the impacts and issues of a United-Continental merger from a congressional perspective. Several major issues associated with the merger are discussed, including its potential effect on airfares, its effect on routes and services, whether employment is likely to increase or decrease, whether existing United-Continental airport hubs will retain their status in the future, how the United-Continental merger will affect further consolidation in the U.S. airline industry, and whether the merger will have a significant impact on industry profitability.

Congress does not have a direct role in the merger approval process, having legislatively charged the executive branch with that task. The authority to approve or disapprove airline mergers rests entirely with DOJ. The Department of Transportation (DOT), and more specifically the Office of the Secretary of Transportation (OST), is a participant in the proceeding and makes recommendations to DOJ based on its evaluation of the effect of a proposed merger on airline industry competition.

Most congressional interest in this proposed merger will likely focus on how it might play out at the district level, in terms of whether service at the local airport will be affected, how it will affect local employment, and other economic effects that could impact the district. Some Members, especially those serving on transportation-related committees, may take a broader view, seeking to ascertain how the merger will affect competition (as measured by factors such as service, fares, and the presence/absence of competing airlines in certain market pairs) nationwide and internationally.

AIRLINE MERGERS/ACQUISITIONS

The May 3, 2010, announcement by United Airlines and Continental Airlines that they would seek authority from the Department of Justice (DOJ) to merge was mostly well received within the aviation industry community. In addition, there also seems to be considerable support for industry consolidation in the financial community and, in some instances, in the press.[1] Nonetheless, there has been opposition to the merger from some quarters. For example, House Committee on Transportation and Infrastructure (T&I) Chairman James Oberstar claims the combination will be "anti-competitive" and should not be allowed.[2] Other interests, such as organized labor, are wary of the merger and seek additional details about the specifics before they will support it.

When combined, the firm will be the world's largest airline by most measures, surpassing Delta Airlines, which currently holds that title by virtue of a 2008 merger/acquisition with Northwest Airlines. A combined United and Continental would command 22% of capacity measured by available seat miles in the U.S. market, compared to Delta's 20% share as shown in Table 1. As a result, over two-fifths of all currently served domestic routes would be flown by either the new United or Delta. The other major airlines in the market by available seat miles are American, Southwest, and US Airways.

Table 1. Capacity of Selected Major U.S. Airlines: 2009 (Thousands)

Airline	Capacity as measured by available seat miles	Capacity as measured by available seat miles
United-Continental	217,166,073	22.3%
Delta	197,701,801	20.3%
American	151,772,114	15.6%
Southwest	98,170,798	10.1%
US Airways	70,721,007	7.3%
Total	975,294,854	

Source: Bureau of Transportation Statistics Form 41 data, httpi/www.transtats.bts.gov.

From a business perspective the merger will, according to its proponents, create annual synergies and efficiencies of over $1 billion by 2013.[3] This may allow the newly minted airline, flying under the United nameplate, to improve service, reduce costs, and become a better global competitor.[4] The merged airlines anticipate generating these savings by cutting overhead, right- sizing their airline fleets, and making their operations more efficient. For the moment, the carriers are suggesting that they will not need to close airport hubs, reduce air service, or lay off large numbers of employees, at least in the short term.[5] One-time consolidation costs (e.g., integrating technologies and harmonizing fleets) are expected to cost $1.2 billion over three years.[6] Opponents of the merger contend that the real effects will be higher fares, reduced service to many localities, laid-off workers, and greater market concentration in an industry where some believe market power is already overly concentrated.

The United-Continental merger announcement came only weeks after it appeared that United would instead merge with a different carrier, US Airways. The merger continues the trend toward consolidation among what are now referred to as "legacy and/or network carriers," and, if approved, would leave only four such large carriers operating in the United States (a newly combined United, Delta, American, and US Airways).[7] The most recent of these prior consolidations was the merger/acquisition of Northwest and Delta under the Delta nameplate in 2008. Interestingly, a United-Continental merger was under discussion at that time, but Continental decided not to pursue the merger largely due to concerns about United's financial health.[8]

In 1978, when economic regulation of the airline industry ended, many opponents of deregulation contended that the large major carriers in the industry would rapidly combine into as few as three airlines, possibly with regional monopoly power. This prediction was obviously off its mark since it has taken 32 years for the consolidation of major carriers to finally occur. In the interim, however, the industry's structure has changed dramatically. Low-cost carriers (LCCs) with nationwide reach and broad market penetration such as Southwest and AirTran did not exist in 1978.[9] Also, the role of regional airlines in the system as feeders to the larger carriers and sometimes as stand alone carriers has increased dramatically.

In looking at today's airline industry it is important to realize that the industry descends from the pre-1978 regulated industry, but by virtue of multiple bankruptcies and other management changes most of the carriers discussed here are related to pre-1978 carriers primarily by name alone. As shown in Figure 1, several major airlines have gone through multiple Chapter 11 bankruptcy reorganizations since 1978; for example, Continental (1983 and 1990) and US Airways (1991, 2002, and 2004, including America West which purchased US Airways in 2005). Most of the major carriers involved in recently approved mergers, and in the now pending merger, have been through the Chapter 11 process in recent years. In addition, a significant number of airlines have been added to the industry and subsequently failed over the last 32 years. Well over 160 airlines, mainly start-up firms not shown in Figure 1 (known in airline terminology as "new entrants"), but also some well known firms, have filed for bankruptcy in the intervening years. In the vast majority of these cases the bankruptcy led ultimately to a departure from the industry.

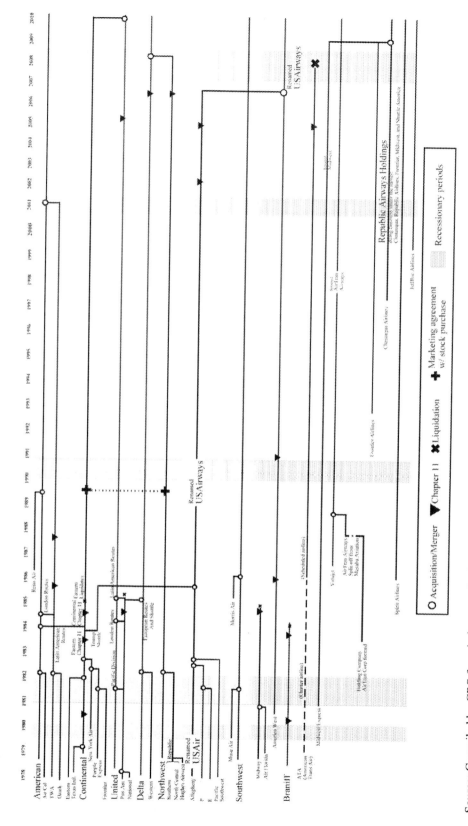

Source: Compiled by CRS from industry and other public sources.

Figure 1. U.S. Airline Industry Consolidation: 1978–Present

At the top of its structure, the airline industry appears to be marching toward consolidation. Two decades ago this would have eliminated much of the competition in the industry. In an industry filled with LCCs and Regionals the potential effects of a merger on competition are more nuanced, requiring a close examination of various market segments. This is especially true when looking at international routes which are still largely dominated by network carriers or their international alliance strategic partners. It is against this backdrop that DOJ must decide whether the United-Continental merger creates competitive and/or antitrust problems. DOJ can approve the merger outright, approve it with conditions (such as route carveouts and airport slot sales/trades), or disapprove it in its entirety.

THE CONGRESSIONAL ROLE

Congress does not have a direct role in the merger approval process, having legislatively charged the executive branch with that task. The authority to approve or disapprove airline mergers rests entirely with the Department of Justice (DOJ).[10] The Office of the Secretary of Transportation (OST) is a participant in the proceeding and makes recommendations to DOJ based on its evaluation of the effect of a proposed merger on airline industry competition.

Most congressional interest in this proposed merger will likely focus on how it might play out at the District level, in terms of whether service at the local airport will be affected, how it will affect local employment, and on other economic effects that could impact Members' districts. Some Members, especially those serving on transportation-related committees, may examine additional issues seeking to ascertain how the merger will affect competition (as measured by factors such as service, fares, and the presence/absence of competing airlines in certain market pairs) nationwide and internationally. These same Members are also likely to be looking at how the merger might affect labor unions, aircraft manufacturers, and a wide range of airline industry suppliers.

During previous merger discussions, individual Members of Congress have taken positions both for and against proposed mergers, hearings have been held, and some legislation has been introduced and considered. Chairman Oberstar and several other Members have already expressed specific concerns about the proposed merger between United and Continental. Members of the Ohio delegation (Representatives Kucinich, Fudge, Kaptur, Sutton, and Tiberi) have publicly voiced their unease about the future of Continental's hub operation in Cleveland and access to air service more generally.[11] Similarly, Representative Shelia Jackson Lee has requested an investigation into the merger. [12] As of this writing, one hearing has been held in the Senate, by the Senate Committee on the Judiciary (May 27, 2010); a hearing scheduled by the Senate Committee on Commerce, Science, and Transportation has been postponed, and a hearing by the House T&I Committee is scheduled for June 16, 2010. Additional hearings on the merger are possible before the end of the 111th Congress.

HISTORICAL PERSPECTIVES

As **Figure 1** shows, post-1978 airline deregulation mergers and acquisitions began occurring in the early to mid-1980s. During that period many of the so-called "local service carriers" of the regulated era, such as Ozark, Republic, Southern, PSA, were combined into larger airlines. A second wave of consolidation occurred in the later 1980s at least in part driven by the availability of "leveraged buyout" (LBO) financing available during the period. The effects of the First Persian Gulf War, which depressed international airline travel for the first time in post-World War II history, put an end to most consolidation discussions, at least for a time.

During the 1980s most congressional interest in mergers seems to have been focused on service issues and on ensuring that airline employees were fairly treated as firms were acquired and/or combined. Members of Congress expressed their views on many of the combinations of that time period. Congressional concern was also expressed about how the merger approval process was exercised at the federal level. Many felt that the Reagan Administration Department of Transportation (DOT) was too friendly to mergers, approving at least two mergers that DOJ had questioned. Ultimately, in response to these concerns, Congress acted to strip DOT of its preeminent role in the merger approval process and moved it to DOJ beginning in 1989.

During the last decade there have been several significant merger/acquisitions and one proposal that was ultimately rejected by DOJ. American's acquisition of TWA (2001) and America West's acquisition of US Airways (2005) were approved without major congressional opposition. In each instance, the airline being acquired (TWA and US Airways) was in significant financial difficulty and the acquisition was viewed by many as a way of preserving jobs and air service. The merger of Delta and Northwest in 2008 under the Delta name created some congressional interest detailed below. A smaller and more recent consolidation, the acquisition of Midwest and Frontier by Republic Airlines Holdings (which is a large regional carrier not associated with the Republic mentioned earlier) attracted little congressional interest.

The rejected merger was a May 2000 proposal by United to acquire US Airways, that engendered considerable public opposition which was very much reflected by many Members of Congress. The merger proposal had some novel features, including a proposal to create a new airline based at Reagan National Airport, and later a link to the American and TWA merger, that was designed to deflect possible anti-trust concerns related to the market power of a combined United and US Airways. These proposals, however, were insufficient to ward off concerns about the anticompetitive nature of the proposed combination. Although there were individual Members of Congress who were in favor of the merger, there seems to have been significantly more congressional opposition to the merger. These anti-merger positions were especially apparent during several hearings held to examine the potential competitive effects of the merger. Although no legislation blocking or otherwise altering the merger was passed, several pieces of legislation that would have impacted the merger were introduced and considered. Ultimately, DOJ would reject the merger in July 2001 and United, deciding not to appeal the ruling, withdrew its offer.

Executives of Delta and Northwest argued in 2008 that their combination was necessary for competitive reasons. In addition to creating what became the nation's largest airline, they believed that the new airline would be "more stable and be better able to grow to meet the challenges of the future" in what they view as the highly competitive world airline industry and a difficult economic environment.[13] From their perspective the new Delta combination would provide synergies that could reduce operating costs by up to $1 billion. As part of their merger, they promised not to close airport hubs, reduce air service, or dismiss large numbers of employees.

Many airline industry observers at the time were dubious of these claims. They found it hard to understand, for example, how a firm that planned not to cut employees, close hubs, etc., would be able to come up with the cost savings stated as the rationale for the merger. In fact, at least some of their skepticism seems well placed. Although Delta has not engaged in wholesale route cutting or staff firing it has, nonetheless, already made some significant changes to its route structure. Cincinnati, for example, is no longer the regional hub it was just a few years ago, with the number of domestic enplaned passengers dropping by more than 50%, from 10.3 million in 2005 to 5 million in 2009.[14]

In 2008, several Members of Congress including House T&I Committee Chairman James Oberstar, and the Chairman of the Subcommittee on Aviation, Jerry Costello opposed the merger and expressed skepticism about the supposed positive aspects of the merger.[15] They did hold hearings on the merger. Those hearings did not influence the outcome of the merger application, which DOJ ultimately approved.

AIRLINE INDUSTRY OVERVIEW

U.S. airlines carried 5.2% fewer domestic passengers in 2009 than in 2008, totaling just over 618 million passengers.[16] This drop in airline customers is one important factor, along with fluctuating fuel costs and a generally weak economy, which has resulted in the volatile financial results posted by the industry in recent years. Both United and Continental posted hefty losses in 2009; revenues were down 19.1% at United (losing $651 million) and 17.4% at Continental (losing $282 million) between 2008 and 2009.[17] Similarly challenging financial problems exist at the other legacy carriers. Analysts at *Airline Forecasts*, an investment research firm, however, predict profits for the major U.S. carriers in 2010 and 2011.[18] Some low-cost carriers, like Southwest and JetBlue, have remained profitable by focusing on keeping costs low and managing their growth; for instance, Southwest reported a net profit for its 37th consecutive year even though its operating revenues were also down year-over-year between 2008 and 2009.[19] From a labor market perspective, employment in the airline industry has declined over the past decade. Airlines shed nearly 135,000 jobs, with direct airline industry employment dropping from 520,600 in 2000 to 386,100 in 2009, based on DOT data.[20]

POTENTIAL UNITED-CONTINENTAL MERGER IMPACTS

Mergers invariably attract attention because they alter the status quo in a way that makes predicting long term consequences difficult. Airline mergers do not always go as planned and/or realize their stated goals. The stock holders, employees, customers, and served communities often have competing interests in the merger process. Some stakeholders may support a merger at the outset of discussions, but change their mind over time, and the reverse, of course, is true.

Airfares

Airline executives historically have claimed that airfares will not rise after a merger. Whether this is the case or not is usually hard to judge, however, because most fare changes occur on a routeby-route basis not on a system-wide basis. A cut in capacity is one of the rationales for a merger, which reduces the number of available airline seats and could, in turn, lead to increased fares. Various industry analysts anticipate that a combined United might cut capacity by reducing the number of available seats anywhere from 5% to 10% nationwide. For example, JP Morgan analysts assume a cut in capacity of 8%.[21] Basic economics would suggest that the same number of passengers seeking a reduced supply of seats will end up paying more for the privilege of flying. In fact, the *Wall Street Journal* reported that "the merger could help stabilize the loss- plagued U.S. industry by taking more seats out of the skies and giving all carriers more leeway to raise fares."[22]

Whether airfares actually rise depends on specific market conditions and whether there is a low- cost alternative, among other factors. For instance, certain types of fares might not change that much because of existing or potential LCC competition. Smaller and regional markets might see an increase in fares because there might not be as much competition in those markets, especially if the market is small and therefore unattractive to an LCC. One analyst found when one airline suddenly dominates a route where it previously competed with a merger partner, ticket prices tend to rise—often considerably.[23] But, if there is a low-cost carrier on that route, fares will be lower. This conclusion was reached based on an examination of airline fares from St. Louis at the time TWA merged with American for the period 2001 to 2008. Similar conclusions have been reached by others. For example, several General Accounting Office (now the Government Accountability Office) (GAO) reports on airline competition found fares at concentrated hubs are higher than fares elsewhere.[24] JP Morgan analysts expect New Orleans, San Diego, Seattle, and Washington, D.C. could experience market concentration as a result of the United-Continental merger, which could possibly result in higher fares in those markets.[25]

Routes and Frequencies

Specific route changes as a result of the merger are also unclear, but almost certainly some routes will be cut. Reducing flight schedules has the potential of affecting entire communities. Even though the two merging airlines maintain there is little route overlap, it seems certain cities may lose service, which could result in fewer flight frequencies and in some cases a loss of non-stop service. According to Continental, minimal domestic overlap exists between the airlines, and all of the nonstop overlap routes have at least one other domestic nonstop competitor. The overlap routes as identified by Continental are: Houston–Washington, Los Angeles, San Francisco, Chicago and Denver; Cleveland–Denver, Chicago and Washington; and, Newark/New York– Denver, Los Angeles, Chicago, San Francisco, and Washington. Low-cost carriers, such as Southwest and JetBlue, are significant competitors on some of these routes. DOJ will examine whether there is sufficient competition on these routes as part of its merger review.

As noted earlier, an issue of importance to many Members of Congress is what might happen to air service in small communities that already have difficulty attracting and maintaining scheduled air service. As airlines continue to reduce capacity, small communities could potentially see even further reductions in service and some cities that currently have direct flights to a hub airport might lose them. In announcing the merger, United and Continental have stated they will continue to serve all the communities each airline now serves, but whether this will be true over the longer term remains questionable.[26]

Airline Employment

One of the biggest and most difficult operational challenges for the combined airline will be the integration of their respective highly unionized workforces, which currently total 88,000 employees (approximately 45% of Continental's full-time equivalent employees and 82% of United's active employees were represented by various unions as of December 31, 2009).[27] If the merger goes forward, the combined company will have to reach agreements with their unions that address pay issues, proscribe job work rules, and determine the process of melding employees of the two airlines into a single workforce which is frequently complicated by seniority issues. United and Continental executives sent a letter to their respective employees stating that "the merger will not have an immediate effect on your job," but that same letter notes that some "local reductions" will occur in the future.[28] No consolidation of the two workforces is expected to happen in the near term, since it will take at least until the first half of 2012 to operationally merge the two carriers, assuming DOJ approves the merger by year-end 2010.

The proposed merger has received a mixed response from the employees of both companies. Most analysts believe that unions representing frontline employees, such as pilots and machinists, will largely determine whether the new United reaches its full potential or whether it is plagued by future labor problems. Unlike the situation at the outset of the Delta merger, no single union contract had been agreed upon ahead of the United-Continental merger announcement, thus their respective unionized workforces are working under open contracts.

The employees of the two carriers are represented by almost identical unions, which include the Airline Pilots Association (ALPA), the Association of Flight Attendants (AFA), the International Association of Machinists and Aerospace Workers (IAM), and the International Brotherhood of Teamsters (IBT). All of these unions have already voiced concerns about the pending merger. Leaders of the Continental and United Airlines chapters of ALPA said they would work with the new management team and they have indicated tentative support for the deal.[29] Other unions have expressed greater skepticism. For instance, IAM, which represents some 26,000 workers at the two airlines, has concerns about the proposed deal, specifically regarding pensions, benefits, seniority, and job security.[30] AFA, which represents 16,000 flight attendants at United, has also publicly voiced their unease about what the merger could mean for them.[31] Whether the unions will be able to obtain acceptable agreements from the merging airlines for their members remains to be seen.

Airport Hubs

The merger partners have said that they expect to keep their eight U.S. hubs open if the merger is approved and have no plans to close any of them. Continental currently operates three domestic hubs (Houston, Newark, and Cleveland) and United has five (Chicago, San Francisco, Denver, Los Angeles, and Washington Dulles). However, industry observers are skeptical that the efficiencies announced by the agreement can be reached without some hub realignment and argue that some hub airports could be at risk if the two airlines merge. As with previous consolidations, there likely could be a deeper impact at some hubs than at others. Some analysts point to examples like the downsizing of TWA's main hub at Lambert–St. Louis Airport, when American bought TWA in 2001. Since then, passenger traffic has declined from 23.5 million in 2002 to fewer than 12 million in 2009.[32] Despite promises to the contrary, it also seems the Delta merger could bring about some hub closures in the near term as the two companies continue melding their operations, possibly from among their four hubs that are viewed by some analysts as being relatively close to each other: Minneapolis, Cincinnati, Memphis, and Detroit.[33]

Given the experience with past mergers, concerns have already been raised by lawmakers as to what might happen at various airport hubs under a merged United-Continental. For instance, whether Continental's Cleveland Hopkins International Airport could remain a hub airport given its market size and proximity to United's Chicago hub seems uncertain over the long term.[34]

Further Industry Consolidation

Of the remaining so-called network/legacy air carriers, the most likely future merger partner is US Airways. US Airways is known to be looking for a partner, especially in the wake of its inability to make its own deal with United prior to the United-Continental announcement. US Airways President Doug Parker spoke at a meeting days before the United announcement explaining the need for fewer legacy airlines by stating, "We didn't need seven of them in 2005.

We don't need four of them now. We need three."[35] The obvious remaining partner would be American Airlines. For the moment, however, American is not pursuing an acquisition or merger, instead stating a preference for focusing itself on profitability rather than expansion.[36] There is also a feeling in the industry that American's purchase of TWA did not work out very well and was essentially a write off, making the firm somewhat reluctant to expand by acquisition or merger.

A major barrier to further consolidation is probably that the track record of airline mergers in the United States is spotty at best. Some airline industry analysts believe that there has never been an undisputedly successful merger in the industry's history.[37] Even those who claim further mergers might be positive question the likelihood that the transition from two airlines to one will be smooth for fliers and employees and ultimately provide true value for the new firms. These critics point to the aforementioned American Airlines acquisition of TWA and the many employee and infrastructure integration problems experienced after American West acquired and took the name US Airways.[38]

There is also a question, in the eyes of some analysts, as to whether the assumed benefits of a merger are worth the hassle of the merger itself. This view derives from the growth of international alliances that allow participating airlines to offer their services in ways that are, in some cases, indistinguishable from those offered by a single firm. United and Continental, for example, are both members of the Star Alliance (as is US Airways). As a result, they already are able to coordinate some of their activities through such practices as code-sharing (the ability of one airline to book service on another airline using its code) and coordination of their frequent- flier programs. This existing and expanding relationship has caused some observers to question the need for greater future consolidation in the industry.

Airline Profitability

The airline industry frequently points out that it has been unprofitable over the long term and especially over the last decade.[39] In part this is because the airline industry as a whole is highly competitive and is viewed by many analysts as being marginally profitable only in its best years. Some carriers have, nonetheless, been mostly or entirely profitable over the long term (most notably Southwest). Proponents of the United-Continental merger, as discussed earlier, contend that efficiencies associated with the merger will enhance the combined firm's profitability and perhaps the profitability prospects of the entire industry. They also argue that the combined firm will be better able to withstand the occasional economic shocks that have recently pushed the industry as a whole into unprofitability, such as the recently ended recession and the oil price volatility of 2008.

Those who question the merger would probably claim that the new United's economic prospects and those of the entire industry will be determined to a large extent by forces, such as fuel prices, over which they will have only marginal control. They would also argue that previous mergers have not protected firms in the industry from economic and political events, and there is no reason to believe mergers, as opposed to good management, whatever the size of the firm, will have a protective effect on an airline's operation.

End Notes

[1] "Our view on airline consolidation: Fewer, but stronger, carriers could benefit fliers," editorial, *USA Today*, May 14, 2010.
[2] "Oberstar Finds United's Merger With Continental Airlines Anti-Competitive," *Aviation Daily*, May 7, 2010, p. 4.
[3] The combined firm had 2009 revenues of approximately $29 billion. See http://www.united continentalmerger.com/benefits/investors.
[4] Mouawad, Jad, and de la Merced, Michael J., "In United-Continental Deal, a Coast-to-Coast Behemoth," *The New York Times*, May 3, 2010.
[5] For more information about the proposed combined company, see http://www.unitedcontinentalmerger.com/combined-company.
[6] "Let's Fly Together," investor presentation, United Airlines, May 3, 2010, p. 20, available at http://www.unitedcontinentalmerger.com/sites/default/files/pdfs/FINAL+Investor+Presentation%5B1%5D.pdf

[7] Historically, airlines were typically classified by DOT as Majors, Nationals, or Regionals based on their market size. In public discussions, however, airlines are now commonly referred to by descriptives such as legacy and/or network carriers, value carriers and/or low-cost carriers (LCCs), and regional carriers. Market size in this categorization is less important than the firm's history and its operational strategy. For example, Southwest, which enplanes more passengers than many of the network carriers, is viewed as an LCC airline because of its low fares and lack of traditional airline hubs.

[8] U.S. Government Accountability Office. *Airline Mergers. Issues Raised by the Proposed Merger of United and Continental Airlines.* GAO-10-7785. May 27, 2010. p. 4. http://www.gao.gov/new.items/d10778t.pdf.

[9] Southwest was an intrastate Texas air carrier at the time of deregulation.

[10] 15 U.S.C. § 18a(d)(1)

[11] Gillispie, Mark, "U.S. Rep. Dennis Kucinich Vows to Ensure that Cleveland is not Harmed by the Merger of Continental and United Airlines," *The Plain Dealer.* May 3, 2010, http://blog.cleveland.com/metro/2010/05/post_277.html.

[12] U.S. Congresswoman Shelia Jackson Lee, "I Do Not Endorse the Proposed Merger between Continental and United Airlines," press release, May 4, 2010, available at http://jacksonlee.house.gov/News/DocumentSingle.aspx? DocumentID=1 84148.

[13] Anderson, Richard, and Steenland, Doug, "Some Myths About Airline Mergers," *The Wall Street Journal*, April 16, 2008, p. A19.

[14] U.S. Department of Transportation, Research and Innovative Technology Administration, http://www.bts.gov/.

[15] "Delta-NWA Merger Obstacles Include Labor, Competition," *Aviation Daily*, April 16, 2008, p. 1.

[16] U.S. Department of Transportation, Research and Innovative Technology Administration, Bureau of Transportation Statistics, "Summary 2009 Traffic Data for U.S. and Foreign Airlines: Total Passengers Down 5.3 Percent from 2008," press release, March 29, 2010, available at http://www.bts.gov /press_releases/2010/bts015_10/html/bts015_10.html.

[17] Company-specific financial data were obtained from Hoover's. http://www.hoovers.com/.

[18] Cordle, Vaughn, Mifsud, Paul, and Bonilla, Carlos, "United + Continental is a Big Win for All Stakeholders," *AirlineForecasts.com*, May 5, 2010.

[19] Southwest Airlines, *2009 Annual Report to Shareholders*, January 29, 2010, pp. 23-24, available at http://www.southwest.com/investor_relations/if_sec_filings.html.

[20] U. S. Department of Transportation, Research and Innovative Technology Administration, Bureau of Transportation Statistics, "February 2010 Passenger Airline Employment down 3.5 Percent from February 2009," press release, April 20, 2010, available at http://www.bts.gov/press_releases/2010/bts019_10/html/bts019_10.html#table_03. Historical employment data to 2000 was provided directly to CRS by BTS staff.

[21] Baker, Jamie. "Airlines: Consolidation Implications; Equity Ratings, Targets, Estimates Revised; Reiterate Credit Overweight," J.P. Morgan, April 19, 2010, p. 7.

[22] Chon, Gina and Carey, Susan, "United Airlines, Continental to Announce Merger," *Wall Street Journal*," May 3, 2010, available at http://online.wsj.com/article/SB10001424052748703969204575220372800747024.html

[23] McGee, Bill, "When Airlines Merge, Consumers Usually Lose," travel column, *USA Today*, April 29, 2009, available at http://www.usatoday.com/travel/columnist/mcgee/2010-04-28-airline-mergers

[24] U.S. General Accounting Office. *Airline Competition: Higher Fares and Less Competition Continue at Concentrated Airports.* GAO/RCED-93-171. July 1993. http://archive.gao.gov/t2pbat5/149695.pdf. U.S. General Accounting Office. *Aviation Competition: Challenges in Enhancing Competition in Dominated Markets.* GAO/01-518T. March 31, 2001. http://www.gao.gov/new.items/d01518t.pdf.

[25] Pender, Kathleen, "United, Continental Merger Could Raise Airfares," *SFGate.com*, May 4, 2010, available at http://articles.sfgate.com/2010-05-04/business/20883109_1_star-alliance-airline-fares-route-system.

[26] United Airlines, " United and Continental Announce Merger of Equals to Create World-Class Global Airlines," press release, May 3, 2010, available at http://www.united.com/press/detail/0,7056,62956,00.html.

[27] These statistics were compiled from the 2009 10-K filings for Continental and United.

[28] Maxon, Terry, "Smisek Tells Continental Employees about the United Merger," *Dallas Morning News*, May 3, 2010, available at http://aviationblog.dallasnews.com/archives/2010/05/smisek-tells-continental-emplo.html.

[29] Air Line Pilots Association, "Statement by Captain Wendy Morse, United Master Executive Council, and Captain Jay Pierce, Chairman, Continental Master Executive Council, Air Line Pilots Association, International, Regarding Merger between United Airlines and Continental Airlines," press release, May 3, 2010, available at http://www.alpa.org/Portals/Alpa/PressRoom/PressReleases/2010/5-3-10_10.UAL-CAL.htm.

[30] International Association of Machinists and Aerospace Workers, "Machinists Warn of Obstacles to UAL/Continental Merger," press release, May 3, 2010, available at http://www.goiam.org/index.php/news/press-releases/7228- machinists-warn-of-obstacles-toualcontinental-merger.

[31] Association of Flight Attendants—CWA, "United Flight Attendants on Merger: Contract and Job Protections Must Come First," press release, May 3, 2010, available at http://www.afanet.org/default.asp?id=1270.

[32] U.S. Department of Transportation. Research and Innovative Technology Administration. Bureau of Transportation Statistics. Data on St. Louis Missouri Lambert International Airport by Total Passengers. http://www.transtats.bts.gov/airports Lambert%20International&carrier= FACTS.

[33] Leocha, Charlie, "Delta Reneges on 'No Hub Closure' Promise, Closes Cincinnati Base," *Consumer Travel*, February 5, 2010, available at http://www.consumertraveler.com/today/delta-reneges-on-no-hub-

[34] Grant, Allison, "Continental-United Merger Threatens Routes at Cleveland Hopkins," *The Plain Dealer*, May 9, 2010, available at http://www.cleveland.com/business/index.ssf/2010/05/continental-united_merger_thre.html.

[35] Jenkins, Holman W. Jr., "Airlines vs. History," *The Wall Street Journal*, May 5, 2010, p. A19.

[36] Mouawad, Jad, "A Waning Star of Air Travel Struggles as a Solo Act," *The New York Times*, May 19, 2010.

[37] Bailey, Jeff, "In the Math of Mergers, Airlines Fail," *The New York Times*, January 17, 2008; McCartney, Scott, "The Middle Seat: What's in a Merger? For Fliers, Not Much—History Doesn't Bode Well For Delta-Northwest Combo; A Legacy of Dropped Routes," *The Wall Street Journal*, April 16, 2008, p. D1.

[38] Reed, Dan, "US Airways highlights drawbacks of consolidation," *USA Today*, March 6, 2008.

[39] For more detailed information about industry profitability, the Air Transport Association (ATA) provides considerable historical and prospective profitability information at http://www.airlines.org/Economics /ReviewOutlook/ Pages_Admin/ReviewOutlook.aspx.

In: Airline Industry Mergers: Background and Issues
Editor: Felix J. Mercado

ISBN: 978-1-61761-993-9
© 2011 Nova Science Publishers, Inc.

Chapter 2

AIRLINE MERGERS: ISSUES RAISED BY THE PROPOSED MERGER OF UNITED AND CONTINENTAL AIRLINES

Susan Fleming

WHY GAO DID THIS STUDY

Earlier this month, United Air Lines (United) and Continental Airlines (Continental) announced plans to merge the two airlines and signed a merger agreement. This follows the acquisition of Northwest Airlines by Delta Air Lines (Delta) in 2008, which propelled Delta to become the largest airline in the United States. This latest merger, if not challenged by the Department of Justice (DOJ), would surpass Delta's merger in scope to create the largest passenger airline in terms of capacity in the United States. The passenger airline industry has struggled financially over the last decade, and these two airlines believe a merger will strengthen them. However, as with any proposed merger of this magnitude, this one will be carefully examined by DOJ to determine if its potential benefits for consumers outweigh the potential negative effects.

At the Committee's request, GAO is providing a statement for the record that describes (1) an overview of the factors that are driving mergers in the industry, (2) the role of federal authorities in reviewing merger proposals, and (3) key issues associated with the proposed merger of United and Continental. To address these objectives, GAO drew from previous reports on the potential effects of the proposed merger between Delta and Northwest and the financial condition of the airline industry, and analyzed Department of Transportation (DOT) airline operating and financial data.

WHAT GAO FOUND

As GAO has previously reported, airlines seek to merge with or acquire other airlines to increase their profitability and financial sustainability, but must weigh these potential benefits against operational costs and challenges. The principal benefits airlines consider are cost reductions—by combining complementary assets, eliminating duplicate activities, and reducing capacity—and increased revenues from higher fares in existing markets and increased demand for more seamless travel to more destinations. Balanced against these potential benefits are operational costs of integrating workforces, aircraft fleets, and systems.

DOJ's antitrust review is a critical step in the airline merger and acquisition process. DOJ uses an integrated analytical framework set forth in the *Horizontal Merger Guidelines* to determine whether the merger poses any antitrust concerns. Under that process, DOJ assesses the extent of likely anticompetitive effects of reducing competition in the relevant markets—in this case, between cities or airports. DOJ further considers the likelihood that airlines entering these markets would counteract any anticompetitive effects. It also considers any efficiencies that a merger or acquisition could bring—for example, consumer benefits from an expanded route network. Finally, it examines whether one of the airlines proposing to merge would fail and its assets exit the market in the absence of a merger.

One of the most important issues in this merger will be its effect on competition in the airline industry. For example, GAO's analysis of 2009 ticket data showed that combining these airlines would result in a loss of one effective competitor (defined as having at least 5 percent of total traffic between airports) in 1,135 markets (called airport pairs) affecting almost 35 million passengers while creating a new effective competitor in 173 airport pairs affecting almost 9.5 million passengers (figure). However, in all but 10 of these airports pairs there is at least one other competitor.

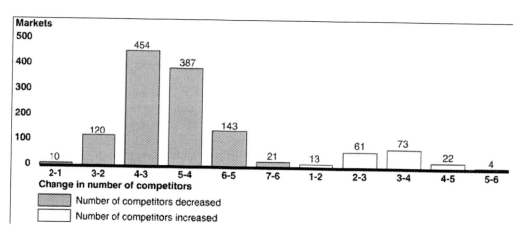

Source: GAO Analysis of DOT Origin and Destintion Ticket Data.

Change in Effective Competitors for Airport-Pair Markets from United-Continental Combination, 2009

Mr. Chairman and Members of the Committee:

We appreciate the opportunity to provide a statement for the record on the potential implications of the merger proposal recently announced by United Air Lines (United) and Continental Airlines (Continental). Earlier this month, these two airlines announced plans for United to merge with Continental through a stock swap the airlines valued at $8 billion. This follows the acquisition of Northwest Airlines (Northwest) by Delta Air Lines (Delta) in 2008, which propelled Delta to become the largest airline in the United States. The United-Continental merger, if not challenged by the Department of Justice (DOJ), would surpass Delta's in scope to create the largest passenger airline in terms of capacity in the United States. However, as with any proposed merger of this magnitude, this one will be carefully examined by DOJ to determine if its potential benefits for consumers outweigh the potential negative effects.

Extensive research and the experience of millions of Americans underscore the benefits that have flowed to most consumers from the 1978 deregulation of the airline industry, including dramatic reductions in fares and expansion of service. These benefits are largely attributable to increased competition from the entry of new airlines into the industry and established airlines into new markets. At the same time, however, airline deregulation has not benefited everyone; some communities—especially smaller communities—have suffered from relatively high airfares and a loss of service. We have been analyzing aviation competition issues since the enactment of the Airline Deregulation Act of 1978.[1] Our work over the last decade has focused on the challenges to competition and industry performance, including the financial health of the airline industry, the growth of low-cost airlines, changing business models of airlines, and prior mergers.[2] In the airline context, DOJ has the primary responsibility to evaluate most mergers in order to carry out its antitrust responsibilities.[3] In its review, DOJ considers a number of factors, including increases in market concentration; potential adverse effects on competition; the likelihood of new entry in affected markets and possible counteraction of anticompetitive effects that the merger may have posed; verified "merger specific" efficiencies or other competitive benefits; and whether, absent the merger, one of the airlines is likely to fail and its assets exit the market.

This statement presents (1) an overview of the factors that are driving mergers in the airline industry, (2) the role of federal authorities in reviewing merger proposals, and (3) key issues associated with the proposed merger of United and Continental. This statement is based on two previously issued reports—our 2008 report for this Committee on airline mergers and our 2009 report on the financial condition of the airline industry and the various effects of the industry's contraction on passengers and communities[4]—as well as our other past work on aviation issues. In addition, we conducted some analysis of the proposed United and Continental merger, including analysis of the airlines' financial, labor, fleet, and market conditions.

To identify the factors that help drive mergers in the airline industry, we relied on information developed for our 2008 and 2009 reports on the airline industry, updated as necessary. To describe the role of federal authorities, in particular DOJ and the Department of Transportation (DOT), in reviewing airline merger proposals we relied on information developed for our 2008 report, also updated as necessary.[5] To identify the key issues associated with the proposed merger of United and Continental, we reviewed airline merger documents and financial analyst reports and analyzed data submitted by the airlines to DOT

(Bureau of Transportation Statistics financial Form 41, origin and destination ticket, and operations data). We also analyzed airline schedule data. We assessed the reliability of these data by (1) performing electronic testing of required data elements, (2) reviewing existing information about the data and the system that produced them, and (3) interviewing agency officials knowledgeable about the data. We determined that the data were sufficiently reliable for the purposes of this chapter. We conducted this audit work in May 2010 in accordance with generally accepted government auditing standards. Those standards require that we plan and perform the audit to obtain sufficient, appropriate evidence to provide a reasonable basis for our findings and conclusions based on our audit objectives. We believe that the evidence obtained provides a reasonable basis for our findings and conclusions based on our audit objectives.

BACKGROUND

On May 3, 2010, United and Continental announced an agreement to merge the two airlines. The new airline would retain the United name and headquarters in Chicago while the current Continental Chief Executive Officer would keep that title with the new airline. The proposed merger will be financed exclusively through an all-stock transaction with a combined equity value of $8 billion split roughly with 55 percent ownership to United shareholders and 45 percent to Continental shareholders. The airlines have not announced specific plans for changes in their networks or operations that would occur if the proposed merger is not challenged by DOJ.

The airline industry has experienced considerable merger and acquisition activity since its early years, especially immediately following deregulation in 1978 (Figure 1 provides a timeline of mergers and acquisitions for the seven largest surviving airlines). A flurry of mergers and acquisitions during the 1980s, when Delta Air Lines and Western Airlines merged, United Airlines acquired Pan Am's Pacific routes, Northwest acquired Republic Airlines, and American Airlines and Air California merged. In 1988, merger and acquisition review authority was transferred from the Department of Transportation (DOT) to DOJ. Since 1998, despite tumultuous financial periods, fewer mergers and acquisitions have occurred. In 2001, American Airlines acquired the bankrupt airline TWA, in 2005 America West acquired US Airways while the latter was in bankruptcy, and, in October 2008, Delta acquired Northwest. Certain other attempts at merging in the last decade failed because of opposition from DOJ or from employees and creditors. For example, in 2000, an agreement was reached that allowed Northwest to acquire a 50 percent stake in Continental (with limited voting power) to resolve the antitrust suit brought by DOJ against Northwest's proposed acquisition of a controlling interest in Continental.[6] A proposed merger of United Airlines and US Airways in 2000 also resulted in opposition from DOJ, which found that, in its view, the merger would violate antitrust laws by reducing competition, increasing air fares, and harming consumers on airline routes throughout the United States. Although DOJ expressed its intent to sue to block the transaction, the parties abandoned the transaction before a suit was filed. More recently, the 2006 proposed merger of US Airways and Delta fell apart because of opposition from Delta's pilots and some of its creditors, as well as its senior management.

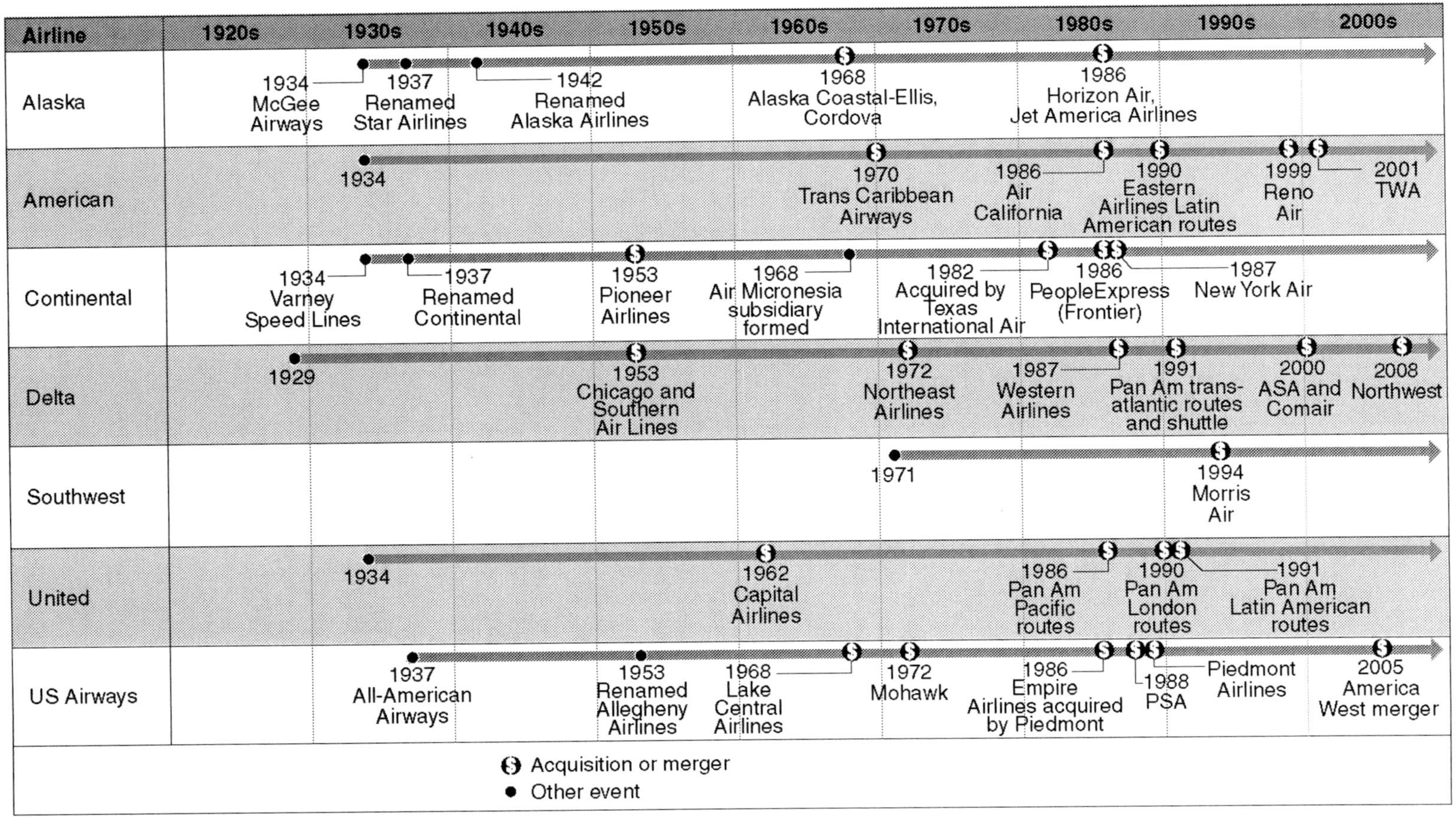

Sources: Cathay Financial and airline company documents.

Figure 1. Highlights of Domestic Airline Mergers and Acquisitions

Since deregulation in 1978, the financial stability of the airline industry has become a considerable concern for the federal government owing, in part, to the level of financial assistance it has provided to the industry by assuming terminated pension plans and other forms of assistance. Between 1978 and 2008, there have been over 160 airline bankruptcies. While most of these bankruptcies affected small airlines that were eventually liquidated, 4 of the more recent bankruptcies (Delta, Northwest, United, and US Airways) are among the largest corporate bankruptcies ever, excluding financial services firms. During these bankruptcies, United and US Airways terminated their pension plans and $9.7 billion in claims was shifted to the Pension Benefit Guarantee Corporation (PGBC).[7] Furthermore, to respond to the shock to the industry from the September 11, 2001, terrorist attacks, the federal government provided airlines with $7.4 billion in direct assistance and authorized $1.6 billion (of $10 billion available) in loan guarantees to six airlines.[8]

Although the airline industry has experienced numerous mergers and bankruptcies since deregulation, growth of existing airlines and the entry of new airlines have contributed to a steady increase in capacity, as measured by available seat miles. Previously, we reported that although one airline may reduce capacity or leave the market, capacity returns relatively quickly.[9] Likewise, while past mergers and acquisitions have, at least in part, sought to reduce capacity, any resulting declines in industry capacity have been short-lived, as existing airlines have expanded or new airlines have expanded. Capacity growth has slowed or declined just before and during recessions, but not as a result of large airline liquidations.

AIRLINE MERGERS ARE DRIVEN BY FINANCIAL AND COMPETITIVE PRESSURES, BUT CHALLENGES EXIST

Volatile earnings and structural changes in the industry have spurred some airlines to explore mergers as a way to increase their profitability and financial viability. Over the last decade, the U.S. passenger airline industry has incurred more than $15 billion in operating losses. Several major airlines went through bankruptcy to reduce their costs and restructure their operations, while others ceased to operate or were acquired. Most recently, U.S. airlines responded to volatile fuel prices and then a weakening economy by cutting their capacity, reducing their fleets and workforces, and instituting new fees, but even with these actions, the airlines experienced over $5 billion in operating losses in 2008 before posting an operating profit of about $1 billion in 2009.[10] Furthermore, over the last decade, airfares have generally declined (in real terms), owing largely to the increased presence of low-cost airlines, such as Southwest Airlines, in more markets and the shrinking dominance of a single airline in many markets.

One of the primary financial benefits that airlines consider when merging with another airline is the cost reduction that may result from combining complementary assets, eliminating duplicative activities, and reducing capacity. A merger or acquisition could enable the combined airline to reduce or eliminate duplicative operating costs, such as duplicative service, labor, and operations costs—including inefficient (or redundant) hubs or routes—or to achieve operational efficiencies by integrating computer systems and similar airline fleets. Other cost savings may stem from facility consolidation, procurement savings, and working capital and balance sheet restructuring, such as renegotiating aircraft leases.

Airlines may also pursue mergers or acquisitions to more efficiently manage capacity—both to reduce operating costs and to generate revenue—in their networks. Given recent economic pressures, particularly increased fuel costs, the opportunity to lower costs by reducing redundant capacity may be especially appealing to airlines seeking to merge. Experts have said that industry mergers and acquisitions could lay the foundation for more rational capacity reductions in highly competitive domestic markets and could help mitigate the significant impact that economic cycles have historically had on airline cash flow.

The other primary financial benefit that airlines consider with mergers and acquisitions is the potential for increased revenues through additional demand, which may be achieved by more seamless travel to more destinations and increased market share and higher fares on some routes.

- *Increased demand from an expanded network*: An airline may seek to merge with or acquire an airline as a way to generate greater revenues from an expanded network, which serves more city-pair markets and better serves passengers. Mergers and acquisitions may generate additional demand by providing consumers more domestic and international city-pair destinations. Airlines with expansive domestic and international networks and frequent flier benefits particularly appeal to business traffic, especially corporate accounts. Results from a recent Business Traveler Coalition (BTC) survey indicate that about 53 percent of the respondents were likely to choose a particular airline based on the extent of its route network.[11] Therefore, airlines may use a merger or acquisition to enhance their networks and gain complementary routes, potentially giving the combined airline a stronger platform from which to compete in highly profitable markets.

- *Increased market share and higher fares on some routes*: Capacity reductions in certain markets after a merger could also serve to generate additional revenue through increased fares on some routes. Some studies of airline mergers and acquisitions during the 1980s showed that prices were higher on some routes from the airline's hubs soon after the combination was completed.[12] Several studies have also shown that increased airline dominance at an airport results in increased fare premiums, in part because of competitive barriers to entry.[13] At the same time, though, even if the combined airline is able to increase prices in some markets, the increase may be transitory if other airlines enter the markets with sufficient presence to counteract the price increase. In an empirical study of airline mergers and acquisitions up to 1992, Winston and Morrison suggest that being able to raise prices or stifle competition does not play a large role in airlines' merger and acquisition decisions.[14]

Cost reductions and the opportunity to obtain increased revenue could bolster a merged airline's financial condition, enabling the airline to better compete in a highly competitive international environment. Many industry experts believe that the United States will need larger, more economically stable airlines to be able to compete with the merging and larger foreign airlines that are emerging in the global economy. The airline industry is becoming increasingly global; for example, the Open Skies agreement between the United States and the European Union became effective in March 2008.[15]

- Despite these benefits, there are several potential barriers to successfully consummating a merger. The most significant operational challenges involve the integration of workforces, aircraft fleets, and information technology systems and processes, which can be difficult, disruptive, and costly as the airlines integrate.

- *Workforce integration*: Workforce integration is often particularly challenging and expensive and involves negotiation of new labor contracts. Labor groups—including pilots, flight attendants, and mechanics—may be able to demand concessions from the merging airlines during these negotiations, several experts explained, because labor support would likely be required for a merger or acquisition to be successful. Some experts also note that labor has often opposed mergers, fearing employment or salary reductions. Obtaining agreement from each airline's pilots' union on an integrated pilot seniority list—which determines pilots' salaries, as well as what equipment they can fly—may be particularly difficult. According to some experts, as a result of these labor integration issues and the challenges of merging two work cultures, airline mergers have generally been unsuccessful. For example, although the 2005 America West–US Airways merger has been termed a successful merger by many industry observers, labor disagreements over employee seniority, and especially pilot seniority, are not fully resolved. More recently, labor integration issues derailed merger talks—albeit temporarily—between Northwest and Delta in early 2008, when the airlines' labor unions were unable to agree on pilot seniority list integration. Furthermore, the existence of distinct corporate cultures can influence whether two firms will be able to merge their operations successfully. For example, merger discussions between United and US Airways broke down in 1995 because the employee-owners of United feared that the airlines' corporate cultures would clash.

- *Fleet integration*: The integration of two disparate aircraft fleets may also be costly. Combining two fleets may increase costs associated with pilot training, maintenance, and spare parts. These costs may, however, be reduced after the merger by phasing out certain types of aircraft from the fleet mix. Pioneered by Southwest Airlines and copied by other low-cost airlines, simplified fleets have enabled airlines to lower costs by streamlining maintenance operations and reducing training times. If an airline can establish a simplified fleet, or "fleet commonality"—particularly by achieving an efficient scale in a particular aircraft—then many of the cost efficiencies of a merger or acquisition may be set in motion by facilitating pilot training, crew scheduling, maintenance integration, and inventory rationalization.

- *Information technology integration*: Finally, integrating information technology processes and systems can also be problematic and time-consuming after a merger. For example, officials at US Airways told us that while some cost reductions were achieved within 3 to 6 months of its merger with America West, the integration of information technology processes took nearly 2 ½ years. Systems integration issues are increasingly daunting as airlines attempt to integrate a complex mix of modern in-house systems, dated mainframe systems, and outsourced information technology. The US Airways-America West merger highlighted the potential challenges associated with combining reservation systems, as there were initial integration problems.

THE DEPARTMENT OF JUSTICE'S ANTITRUST REVIEW IS A CRITICAL STEP IN THE AIRLINE MERGER AND ACQUISITION PROCESS

DOJ's review of airline mergers and acquisitions is a key step for airlines hoping to consummate a merger. For airlines, as with other industries, DOJ uses an analytical framework set forth in the *Horizontal Merger Guidelines* (the Guidelines) to evaluate merger proposals.[17] In addition, DOT plays an advisory role for DOJ and, if the combination is consummated, may conduct financial and safety reviews of the combined entity under its regulatory authority.

Most proposed airline mergers or acquisitions must be reviewed by DOJ as required by the Hart-Scott-Rodino Act. In particular, under the act, an acquisition of voting securities or assets above a set monetary amount must be reported to DOJ (or the Federal Trade Commission (FTC) for certain industries) so the department can determine whether the merger or acquisition poses any antitrust concerns.[18] To analyze whether a proposed merger or acquisition raises antitrust concerns—whether the proposal will create or enhance market power or facilitate its exercise[19]—DOJ follows an integrated five-part analytical process set forth in the Guidelines.[20] First, DOJ defines the relevant product and geographic markets in which the companies operate and determines whether the merger is likely to significantly increase concentration in those markets. Second, DOJ examines potential adverse competitive effects of the merger, such as whether the merged entity will be able to charge higher prices or restrict output for the product or service it sells. Third, DOJ considers whether other competitors are likely to enter the affected markets and whether they would counteract any potential anticompetitive effects that the merger might have posed. Fourth, DOJ examines the verified "merger specific" efficiencies or other competitive benefits that may be generated by the merger and that cannot be obtained through any other means. Fifth, DOJ considers whether, absent the merger or acquisition, one of the firms is likely to fail, causing its assets to exit the market. The commentary to the Guidelines makes clear that DOJ does not apply the Guidelines as a step-by-step progression, but rather as an integrated approach in deciding whether the proposed merger or acquisition would create antitrust concerns.

In deciding whether the proposed merger is likely anticompetitive DOJ considers the particular circumstances of the merger as it relates to the Guidelines' five-part inquiry. The greater the potential anticompetitive effects, the greater must be the offsetting verifiable efficiencies for DOJ to clear a merger. However, according to the Guidelines, efficiencies almost never justify a merger if it would create a monopoly or near monopoly. If DOJ concludes that a merged airline threatens to deprive consumers of the benefits of competitive air service, then it will seek injunctive relief in a court proceeding to block the merger from being consummated. In some cases, the parties may agree to modify the proposal to address anticompetitive concerns identified by DOJ—for example, selling airport assets or giving up slots at congested airports—in which case DOJ ordinarily files a complaint with the court along with a consent decree that embodies the agreed-upon changes.

DOT conducts its own analyses of airline mergers and acquisitions. While DOJ is responsible for upholding antitrust laws, DOT conducts its own competitive analysis and provide it to DOJ in an advisory capacity. DOT reviews the merits of any airline merger or acquisition and submits its views and relevant information in its possession to DOJ. DOT also provides some essential data that DOJ uses in its review.. In addition, presuming the merger moves forward after DOJ review, DOT can undertake several other reviews if the situation warrants. Before commencing operations, any new, acquired, or merged airlines must obtain separate authorizations from DOT—"economic" authority from the Office of the Secretary and "safety" authority from the Federal Aviation Administration (FAA). The Office of the Secretary is responsible for deciding whether applicants are fit, willing, and able to perform the service or provide transportation. To make this decision, the Secretary assesses whether the applicants have the managerial competence, disposition to comply with regulations, and financial resources necessary to operate a new airline. FAA is responsible for certifying that the aircraft and operations conform to the safety standards prescribed by the Administrator— for instance, that the applicants' manuals, aircraft, facilities, and personnel meet federal safety standards. Also, if a merger or other corporate transaction involves the transfer of international route authority, DOT is responsible for assessing and approving all transfers to ensure that they are consistent with the public interest.[21]

In Creating the Largest U.S. Passenger Airline, a United-Continental Merger May Face Integration Challenges and Analysis of Some Overlapping Markets

If not challenged by DOJ, the merged United-Continental would surpass Delta as the largest U.S. passenger airline. As table 1 indicates, combining United and Continental Airlines would create the largest U.S. airline based on 2009 capacity as measured by available seat miles, and a close second based on total assets and operating revenue. The combined airline would also have the largest workforce among U.S. airlines based on March 2010 employment statistics, with a combined 76,900 employees as measured by full-time-equivalent employees (table 2). The airlines' workforces are represented by various unions, and in some cases the same union represents similar employee groups, such as the union for the pilots (table 3). Finally, the combined airline would need to integrate 692 aircraft (table 4). The two airlines share some of the same aircraft types, which could make integration easier.

Table 1. Total Assets, Operating Revenue, and Capacity of Major U.S. Airlines (2009)

	Capacity as measured by available seat miles (thousands)	Total assets	Total operating revenue
United-Continental	217,166,074	$125,742,402	$28,720,624
Delta	197,701,800	195,546,148	28,909,882
American	151,772,113	89,629,364	19,898,245
Southwest	98,170,797	55,190,553	10,350,338
US Airways	70,721,007	28,901,241	10,780,838
Airtran	23,304,612	8,649,482	2,341,442
Alaska	23,148,960	18,045,385	3,005,999

Source: GAO analysis of Bureau of Transportation Statistics Form 41 data.

Table 2. Full-Time-Equivalent Employees of Top U.S. Airlines (March 2010)

Rank	Airline	Total full-time-equivalent employees (thousands)
1	Delta	74.7
2	American[a]	75.2
3	United	43.7
4	Southwest	34.6
5	Continental	33.2
6	US Airways	29.5
7	JetBlue	11.2
8	Alaska	9.2

Source: GAO analysis of Bureau of Transportation Statistics data.
[a]Includes American Eagle.

Table 3. Union Representation for Various Employee Groups

	Employee groups				
	Pilots	**Flight attendants**	**Mechanics**	**Public contact, ramp and stores, and other workers**	**Dispatchers**
United	Air Line Pilots Association (ALPA)	Association of Flight Attendants (AFA)	International Brotherhood of Team-sters (IBT)	International Association of Machinists (IAM)	Professional Airline Flight Control Association (PAFCA)
	Pilots	**Flight attendants**	**Mechanics**	**Fleet service**	**Ticket agents**	**Dispatchers**
Continental	ALPA	IAM	IBT	IBT	Nonunion	Transport Workers Union (TWU)

Source: United Air Lines and Continental Airlines.
Note: In addition, The International Federation of Professional and Technical Engineers (IFPTE) represent more than 260 United engineers and related employees.

Table 4. United and Continental Aircraft Fleet

Aircraft	United	Continental	Merged
Boeing 737		226	226
Boeing 747	24		24
Boeing 757	96	61	157
Boeing 767	35	26	61
Boeing 777	52	20	72
Airbus 319/320	152		152
Total	**359**	**333**	**692**

Source: United Air Lines.

If not challenged by DOJ, the airlines would attempt to combine two distinct networks, United with major hubs, where the airline connects traffic feeding from smaller airports, in San Francisco (SFO), Los Angeles (LAX), Denver (DEN), Chicago O'Hare (ORD), and

Washington DC Dulles (IAD) and Continental with hubs in Houston Intercontinental (IAH), Cleveland (CLE), Guam (GUM), and New York Newark (EWR), as shown in figure 2.

The amount of overlap in airport-pair combinations between the two airlines' networks is considerable if considering all connecting traffic; however, for most of the overlapping airport-pair markets there is at least one other competitor. Based on 2009 ticket sample data, for 13,515 airport pairs with at least 520 passengers per year, there would be a loss of one effective competitor in 1,135 airport-pair markets[22] affecting almost 35 million passengers by merging these airlines (see Figure 3).[23] However, only 10 of these airport-pair markets would not have any other competitors in it after a merger. In addition, any effect on fares would be dampened by the presence of a low-cost airline in 431 of the 1,135 airport pairs losing a competitor.[24] The combination of the two airlines would also create a new effective competitor in 173 airport-pair markets affecting almost 9.5 million passengers.

In examining nonstop overlapping airport pairs between United and Continental, the extent of overlap is less than for connecting traffic. However, the loss of a competitor in these nonstop markets is also more significant because nonstop service is typically preferred by some passengers. For example, based on January 2010 traffic data, the two airlines overlap on 12 nonstop airport-pair routes, which are listed in figure 4.[25] For 7 of these 12 nonstop overlapping airport-pair routes (generally between a United hub and a Continental hub), there are currently no other competitors. However, of these 7 airport-pair markets, all but the Cleveland-Denver market may have relevant competition between other airports in at least one of the endpoint cities. For example, passengers traveling from San Francisco (SFO) to Newark (EWR) could consider airlines serving other airports at both endpoints—Oakland or San Jose instead of SFO and John F. Kennedy (JFK) or LaGuardia instead of EWR.

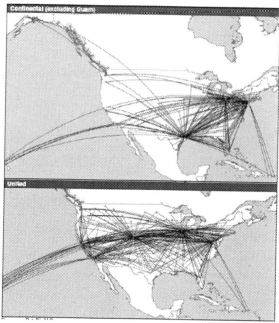

Source: agpDat, Diio LLC.

Figure 2. United and Continental Domestic Route Maps (May 2010)

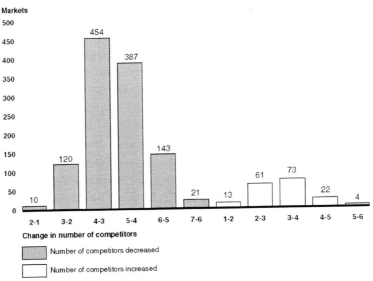

Source: GAO Analysis of DOT Origin and Destination Ticket Data.
Note: All origin and destination airport pairs with at least 520 passengers. A competitor holds at least 5 percent of market share.

Figure 3. Change in Effective Competition from United-Continental Combination (2009)

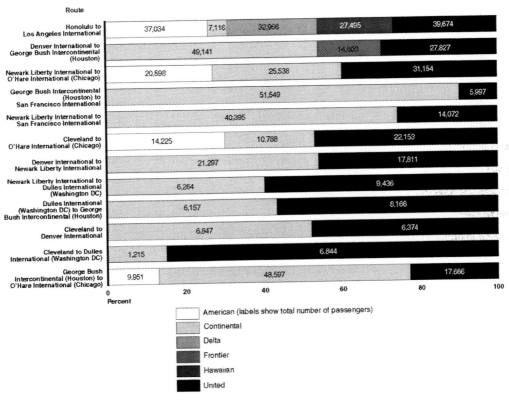

Source: DOT T-100 data.

Figure 4. Total Passengers on Overlapping Nonstop Airport Pairs (January 2010)

Table 5. Passenger Market Share at Hub Airports (2009)

Continental hub airports	Continental share (%)	United hub airports	United share (%)	Total (%)
Houston (IAH)	72		5	77
Newark (EWR)	68		5	73
Cleveland (CLE)	53		6	59
	1	Washington Dulles (IAD)	51	52
	4	Chicago (ORD)	38	42
	6	San Francisco (SFO)	33	39
	4	Denver (DEN)	29	33
	6	Los Angeles (LAX)	17	23

Source: GAO analysis of DOT Origin and Destination ticket data.

If not challenged by DOJ, the combined airline could be expected to rationalize its network over time, including where it maintains hubs. Currently, the two airlines do not have much market share that overlaps at their respective hubs (see table 5). However, it is uncertain whether the combined airline would retain eight domestic hubs. There is considerable overlap between markets served by United out of Chicago (ORD) and Continental out of Cleveland (CLE). For example, 52 out of 62 domestic airports served by Continental from Cleveland are also served by United from Chicago (ORD).

Both United and Continental have extensive world wide networks and serve many international destinations. Between the two airlines, over 100 international cities are served from the United States. The two airlines do not directly compete on a city-to-city route basis for any international destinations. Nevertheless, for international routes, airlines aggregate traffic from many domestic locations at a hub airport where passengers transfer onto international flights. In other words, at Newark, where Continental has a large hub, passengers traveling from many locations across the United States onto Continental's international flights. Likewise, United aggregates domestic traffic at its Washington Dulles hub for many of its international flights. Hence, a passenger traveling from, for example Nashville, may view these alternative routes to a location in Europe as substitutable. Continental and United serve many of the same international destinations in Europe and the Americas from their Newark and Dulles hubs, respectively. These destinations include Amsterdam, Brussels, Frankfort, London, Montreal, Paris, Rome, Sao Paulo, and Toronto. Similarly, both airlines also serve many international destinations from their Midwest hubs— most notably United's hub at Chicago and Continental's hub at Houston. Such destinations include Amsterdam, Cancun, Edmonton, London, Paris, San Jose Cabo, Tokyo, and Vancouver. In total, according to current schedules, they serve 30 common international destinations, representing 65 percent of their total international seat capacity. Whether service to international destinations from different domestic hubs will be viewed as a competitive concern will likely depend on a host of factors, such as the two airlines' market share of traffic to that destination and whether there are any barriers to new airlines entering or existing airlines expanding service at the international destination airports.

To compete internationally, both Continental and United are part of the Star Alliance, one of the three major international airline alliances.[26] In 2009, Continental left the SkyTeam Alliance and joined the Star Alliance. As part of joining this alliance, the Star Alliance members, including Continental, applied for antitrust immunity, which allows the member airlines to coordinate schedules, capacity, and pricing in selected markets. DOT has authority to approve these antitrust immunity applications,[27] but DOJ may also comment if it has antitrust concerns. On June 26, DOJ filed comments that objected to immunity for the alliance in some markets and requested some conditions, called carve-outs, in which the immunity would not be granted. On July 10, 2009, DOT approved the Star Alliance application for antitrust immunity but with special conditions, including carve-outs.[28] Among the markets not granted immunity were New York-Copenhagen, New York-Lisbon, New York-Geneva, New York-Stockholm, Cleveland-Toronto, Houston-Calgary, Houston-Toronto, New York-Ottawa, and U.S.-Beijing.[29]

RELATED GAO PRODUCTS

Airline Industry: Airline Industry Contraction Due to Volatile Fuel Prices and Falling Demand Affects Airports, Passengers, and Federal Government Revenues. GAO-09-393. Washington, D.C.: April 21, 2009.

Airline Industry: Potential Mergers and Acquisitions Driven by Financial Competitive Pressures. GAO-08-845. Washington, D.C.: July 31, 2008.

Commercial Aviation: Bankruptcy and Pension Problems Are Symptoms of Underlying Structural Issues. GAO-05-945. Washington, D.C.: September 30, 2005.

Commercial Aviation: Preliminary Observations on Legacy Airlines' Financial Condition, Bankruptcy, and Pension Issues. GAO-05-835T. Washington, D.C.: June 22, 2005.

Airline Deregulation: Reregulating the Airline Industry Would Likely Reverse Consumer Benefits and Not Save Airline Pensions. GAO-06-630. Washington, D.C.: June 9, 2005.

Private Pensions: Airline Plans' Underfunding Illustrates Broader Problems with the Defined Benefit Pension System. GAO-05-108T. Washington, D.C.: October 7, 2004.

Commercial Aviation: Legacy Airlines Must Further Reduce Costs to Restore Profitability. GAO-04-836. Washington, D.C.: August 11, 2004.

Transatlantic Aviation: Effects of Easing Restrictions on U.S.-European Markets. GAO-04-835. Washington, D.C.: July 21, 2004.

Commercial Aviation: Despite Industry Turmoil, Low-Cost Airlines Are Growing and Profitable. GAO-04-837T. Washington, D.C.: June 3, 2004.

Commercial Aviation: Financial Condition and Industry Responses Affect Competition. GAO-03-171T. Washington, D.C.: October 2, 2002.

Commercial Aviation: Air Service Trends at Small Communities since October 2000. GAO-02-432. Washington, D.C.: March 29, 2002.

Proposed Alliance Between American Airlines and British Airways Raises Competition Concerns and Public Interest Issues. GAO-02-293R. Washington, D.C: December 21, 2001.

Aviation Competition: Issues Related to the Proposed United Airlines-US Airways Merger. GAO-01-212. Washington, D.C: December 15, 2000.

End Notes

[1] Pub. L. No. 95-504, 92 Stat. 1705.

[2] A list of related GAO products is attached to this statement.

[3] Under the Hart-Scott-Rodino Act, an acquisition of voting securities and/or assets above a set monetary amount must be reported to DOJ (or the Federal Trade Commission for certain industries) so the department can determine whether the merger or acquisition poses any antitrust concerns. 15 U.S.C. § 18a(d)(1). Both DOJ and the Federal Trade Commission have antitrust enforcement authority, including reviewing proposed mergers and acquisitions. DOJ is the antitrust enforcement authority charged with reviewing proposed mergers and acquisitions in the airline industry.

[4] GAO, *Airline Industry: Potential Mergers and Acquisitions Driven by Financial and Competitive Pressures*, GAO-08-845 (Washington, D.C.: July 31, 2008); and *Commercial Aviation: Airline Industry Contraction Due to Volatile Fuel Prices and Falling Demand Affects Airports, Passengers, and Federal Government Revenues*, GAO-09-393 (Washington, D.C.: Apr. 21, 2009).

[5] GAO-08-845.

[6] GAO, *Aviation Competition: Issues Related to the Proposed United Airlines-US Airways Merger*, GAO-01-212 (Washington, D.C.: Dec. 15, 2000) p. 10, footnote 6.

[7] PBGC was established under the Employee Retirement Income Security Act of 1974 (ERISA) and set forth standards and requirements that apply to defined benefit plans. PBGC was established to encourage the continuation and maintenance of voluntary private pension plans and to insure the benefits of workers and retirees in defined benefit plans should plan sponsors fail to pay benefits. PGBC operations are financed, for example, by insurance premiums paid by sponsors of defined benefit plans, investment income, assets from pension plans trusted by PBGC, and recoveries from the companies formerly responsible for the plans.

[8] The six airlines receiving loan guarantees were Aloha, World, Frontier, US Airways, ATA, and America West.

[9] GAO, *Commercial Aviation: Bankruptcy and Pensions Problems Are Symptoms of Underlying Structural Issues*, GAO-05-945 (Washington, D.C.: Sept. 30, 2005).

[10] Collectively, U.S. airlines reduced domestic capacity, as measured by the number of seats flown, by about 12 percent from the fourth quarter of 2007 to the fourth quarter of 2009. As we reported in April 2009, to reduce capacity, airlines reduced the overall number of active aircraft in their fleets by eliminating mostly older, less fuel-efficient, and smaller (50 or fewer seats) aircraft. Airlines also collectively reduced their workforces by about 38,000 full-time-equivalent positions, or about 9 percent, from the first quarter of 2008 to the first quarter of 2010. In addition to reducing capacity, most airlines instituted new fees, such as those for checked baggage, which resulted in $3.9 billion in added revenue during 2008 and 2009.

[11] Respondents were travel managers responsible for negotiating and managing their firms' corporate accounts.

[12] See Severin Borenstein, "Airline Mergers, Airport Dominance, and Market Power," *American Economic Review*, Vol. 80, May 1990, and Steven A. Morrison, "Airline Mergers: A Longer View," *Journal of Transport Economics and Policy*, September 1996; and Gregory J. Werden, Andrew J. Joskow, and Richard L. Johnson, "The Effects of Mergers on Price and Output: Two Case Studies from the Airline Industry," *Managerial and Decision Economics*, Vol. 12, October 1991.

[13] See Severin Borenstein, 1989, "Hubs and High Fares: Dominance and Market Power in the U.S. Airline Industry," *RAND Journal of Economics*, 20, 344-365; GAO, *Airline Deregulation: Barriers to Entry Continue to Limit Competition in Several Key Markets*, GAO/RCED-97-4 (Washington, D.C.: Oct. 18, 1996); GAO, *Airline Competition: Effects of Airline and Market Concentration and Barriers to Entry on Airfares*, GAO/RCED-91-101 (Washington, D.C.: Apr. 16, 1991).

[14] See Steven A. Morrison, and Clifford Winston, "The Remaining Role for Government Policy in the Deregulated Airline Industry." *Deregulation of Network Industries: What's Next?* Sam Peltzman and Clifford Winston, eds. Washington, D.C., Brookings Institution Press, 2000 pp. 1-40.

[15] Open Skies seeks to enable greater access of U.S. airlines to Europe, including expanded rights to pick up traffic in one country in Europe and carry it to another European or third country (referred to as fifth freedom rights). Additionally, the United States will expand EU airlines' rights to carry traffic from the United States to other countries.

[16] Airlines also face potential challenges to mergers and acquisitions from DOJ's antitrust review, which is discussed in the next section.

[17] The Guidelines were jointly developed by DOJ's Antitrust Division and the Federal Trade Commission and describe the inquiry process the two agencies follow in analyzing proposed mergers. The most current version of the Guidelines was issued in 1992; Section 4, relating to efficiencies, was revised in 1997. DOJ has proposed some changes in the Guidelines to better reflect its merger review process and the public comment period on these changes has been extended to June 4, 2010.

[18] See 15 U.S.C. § 18a(d)(1). Both DOJ and FTC have antitrust enforcement authority, including reviewing proposed mergers and acquisitions. DOJ is the antitrust enforcement authority charged with reviewing proposed mergers and acquisitions in the airline industry. Additionally, under the Hart-Scott-Rodino Act, DOJ

has 30 days after the initial filing to notify companies that intend to merge whether DOJ requires additional information for its review. If DOJ does not request additional information, the firms can close their deal (15 U.S.C. § 18a(b)). If more information is required, however, the initial 30-day waiting period is followed by a second 30-day period, which starts to run after both companies have provided the requested information. Companies often attempt to resolve DOJ competitive concerns, if possible, before the second waiting period expires. Any restructuring of a transaction—e.g., through a divestiture—is included in a consent decree entered by a court, unless the competitive problem is unilaterally fixed by the parties before the waiting period expires (called a "fix-it first").

[19] Market power is the ability to maintain prices profitably above competitive levels for a significant period of time.

[20] United States Department of Justice and Federal Trade Commission, *Horizontal Merger Guidelines* (Washington, D.C., rev. Apr. 8, 1997).

[21] 49 U.S.C. § 41105. DOT must specifically consider the transfer of certificate authority's impact on the financial viability of the parties to the transaction and on the trade position of the United States in the international air transportation market, as well as on competition in the domestic airline industry.

[22] It is generally preferable, time permitting, to assess city-pair, rather than airport-pair, changes in competition. Some larger U.S. cities (New York, Chicago, Los Angeles, Washington D.C.) have more than one commercial airport that can compete for passenger traffic. DOJ generally considers the relevant market to be a city-pair combination.

[23] For this airport-pair analysis, we considered any airport-pair market with less than 520 annual passengers to be too small to ensure accuracy. We defined an effective competitor as having at least 5 percent of total airport-pair traffic. This is the same minimum market share that we have previously applied to assess whether an airline has sufficient presence in a market to affect competition. See GAO-08-845, p. 21 and 42.

[24] We defined low-cost airlines as JetBlue, Frontier/Midwest, AirTran, Allegiant, Spirit, Sun Country, and Southwest.

[25] In March 2010, Continental initiated nonstop service between Los Angeles (LAX) and Kahului Airport (OGG) in Hawaii, which is also served by United. This compares to 12 nonstop overlaps (7 highly concentrated) in the Delta-Northwest merger.

[26] An airline alliance is an agreement between two or more airlines to cooperate on a substantial level. The three largest passenger airline alliances are the *Star Alliance*, *SkyTeam* and *Oneworld*. Alliances provide a network of connectivity and convenience for international passengers. Alliances also provide a marketing brand to passengers making interairline codeshare connections within countries.

[27] 49 U.S.C. §§ 41308, 41309.

[28] Department of Transportation, Joint Application of Air Canada, et al., Final Order, to Amend Order 2007-2-16 under 49 U.S.C. §§ 41308, 41309, DOT-OST-2008-0234 (July 10, 2009).

[29] In addition, the order modified and placed conditions on pre-existing carve outs for this alliance.

In: Airline Industry Mergers: Background and Issues
Editor: Felix J. Mercado

ISBN: 978-1-61761-993-9
© 2011 Nova Science Publishers, Inc.

Chapter 3

STATEMENT OF SUSAN L. KURLAND, ASSISTANT SECRETARY FOR AVIATION & INTERNATIONAL AFFAIRS, U.S. DEPARTMENT OF TRANSPORTATION, BEFORE THE COMMITTEE ON COMMERCE, SCIENCE & TRANSPORTATION, HEARING ON "THE FINANCIAL STATE OF THE AIRLINE INDUSTRY AND THE IMPLICATIONS OF CONSOLIDATION"

Chairman Rockefeller, Ranking Member Hutchison, and Members of the Committee:

INTRODUCTION

I appreciate the opportunity to appear before you to discuss the current and future state of the airline industry and the role of the Department of Transportation (DOT) in the industry's ongoing restructuring. This hearing isin response to the proposed United/Continentalmerger, a potential combination that has understandably captured the interest of this Committee and the American people.

STATE OF THE AIRLINE INDUSTRY

Let me begin with a brief overview of the state of the airline industryto provide an understanding of the economic environment in which this transaction has been proposed. In the more than 30 years since deregulation, market forces have shaped airline fares and services. During that time, the industry adjusted to a deregulated environment and changing market conditions, facing the expected – fluctuations in supply and demand – but also the unexpected – terrorist attacks, epidemics, and now, with volcanic ash, a natural disaster. Through the various business cycles, carriers have taken steps to cut costs, manage capacity, and cope with volatile fuel prices. Many have adapted well, but not all have succeeded, with an unfortunate number having to file for bankruptcy protection and several exiting the industry altogether.

Following several consecutive years of losses from 2001 to 2005, the industry returned to modest profitability in 2006 and 2007, only to confront rapidly increasing fuel costs and then a global recession. 2008 and 2009 were some of the most challenging years in the history of U.S. aviation, primarily because the global recession helped push operating revenues for the nine largest U.S. airlines down an unprecedented 17% year-over-year. While costs also increased significantly during the first quarter of 2010, airline revenues continue to rebound in large part on the basis of increased passenger volumes.

Each one of the nine largest U.S. carriers increased their revenue, year-over-year, despite the fact that all but one of them decreased or held capacity constant. For the first quarter, the nine largest airlines, whose revenue totaled nearly $27 billion, collectively earned a small operating profit of $17 million, excluding special items. While modest, that representeda substantial improvement from the total operating loss of over $1 billion during the first quarter of 2009.

For thesecond quarter of 2010, most analysts are predicting stronger results, as passenger and shipper demand that vanished during the height of the global recession is returning across all sectors for all carriers. The turn-around from this time last year is encouraging.

Consumers have reaped enormous benefits in the more than 30 years since airline deregulation. During this period, air transportation has been transformed from a luxury thatfew could afford , to a service that provides average families and small businesses of America with affordable access to destinations across the globe. Adjusted for inflation, air fares have continued to decline throughout the deregulated era, as new carriers, particularly low cost carriers, have entered the market and business models of new entrants and incumbent carriers alike have adapted to meet changing consumer needs and brought innovations and efficiencies to the marketplace. In expanding consumer and business access from local to global, air transportation has become an important driver of economic progress for the citizens and companies of this increasingly mobile nation.

We foresee the industry continuing to evolve along several basic trends. First, carriers, while conscious of costs, are aggressively pursuing new sources of revenue. Second, over time, low-cost carriers have expanded significantly. Third, legacy carriers are continuing to seek ways to become more efficient producers, including through stronger alliance partnerships.

DOT's AUTHORITY TO REVIEW MERGER TRANSACTIONS

I am sure you understand that I cannot discuss the specifics of the proposed United/Continental merger, or any proposed transaction that is before us for review. However, I would liketo shed some light on DOT's role in the review of an airline merger.

The Department of Justice (DOJ) has the lead role in reviewing proposed airline mergers, given its statutory authority to enforce the antitrust laws. Utilizing its special aviation expertise, DOT typically examines the proposed merger and shares its analysis and views with the Antitrust Division. This practice is consistent with Congress' determination that the deregulated airline industry should generally be subject to the same application of the antitrust laws as other unregulated industries. Each transaction we review is considered on a case-by-case basis consistent with anti-trust principles and practice.

The purpose of our antitrust laws is to ensurethat consumers receive the benefits of competition , and this is the prism through which the Department analyzes airline mergers. I can therefore assure you that the Department is committed to fostering an environment that embraces competition and provides consumers with the price and service benefits that competition brings.

We also recognize that the airline industry is very dynamic. Cyclical economic conditions, the competitive environment, infrastructureaccess and capacity, and industry innovation all need to be taken into account to allow the industry to adapt to rapidly changing economic conditions.

Should DOJ decide not to challenge a particular transaction on antitrust grounds, DOT would then consider a wide range of follow-on issues that fall within its jurisdiction, including international route transfers, economic fitness, code-sharing, and possible unfair or deceptive practices.

As to international routes, the carriers would be expected to apply for DOT approval of a route transfer to consolidate the international routes they individually hold under one certificate as part of the merger process. By statute (49 U.S.C. 41105), DOT may approve a transfer of such routes only if we find that itis consistent with the public interest. As part ofthat analysis we must examine the transfer's impact on the viability of each airline party to the transaction, competition in the domestic airline industry, and the trade position of the United States in the international air transportation market.

We would only decide aninternational route transfer case after we had established a formal record and given all interested persons the opportunity to comment. If DOT determines that the transfer would be contrary to the public interest on competitive grounds or for another reason, DOT could disapprove the transfer in whole or in part. Alternatively, DOT may condition its approval on requirements that would protect the public interest.

Because a proposed merger of major carriers would involve a significant change in the structure of at least one of the existing carriers, DOT would institute a fitness review of airline management, financials and compliance disposition.

While the transfer application is pending, the merging carriers could request that DOT grant them an exemption from the provisions of 49 U.S.C. 41105 to allow them to consummate the merger at their own risk pending DOT's decision on their transfer application. DOT has sometimes approved such exemption requests in the past, conditioned upon the air carriers remaining separate and independently operated entities under common ownership until the transfer application case is decided.

DOT may also review any code-share arrangements concluded between the merging carriers. In DOT's experience, code-share arrangements would likely be necessary during the early phases of integration after the transaction is closed.

Finally, at DOT, we take our responsibility for consumer protection seriously. For example, if carriers in pursuing or implementing a merger were to engage in unfair or deceptive practices, we would not hesitate to act to protect affected consumers based on our 49 U.S.C. 41712 authority.

CONCLUSION

Airlines are the circulatory system of national and global communities – linking friends and family, suppliers and producers, retailers and manufacturers, facilitating business partnerships, and fostering educational and cultural exchanges of all types. Every American has both a personal and an economic interest in access to safe and affordable air travel. It is therefore easy to understand why so many people take an interest in airline mergers.

Our consideration of aviation economic policy focuseson what is best for a hea lthy and a competitive industry, for its workers, and for the communities and consumers that it serves. Our goal must be to strike what is oftena very difficult balance in the face of a complex and dynamically changing industry. Importantly, in doing so we must also consider the longer term, collective impact on all stakeholders, most importantly America's traveling public.

Mr. Chairman, this concludes my testimony. I would be happy to answer any questions you may have.

In: Airline Industry Mergers: Background and Issues
Editor: Felix J. Mercado

ISBN: 978-1-61761-993-9
© 2011 Nova Science Publishers, Inc.

Chapter 4

JOINT STATEMENT OF GLENN F. TILTON, CHAIRMAN, PRESIDENT AND CEO, UAL CORP., AND JEFFERY SMISEK, CHAIRMAN, PRESIDENT AND CEO, CONTINENTAL AIRLINES, INC., BEFORE THE COMMITTEE ON COMMERCE, SCIENCE & TRANSPORTATION, HEARING ON "THE FINANCIAL STATE OF THE AIRLINE INDUSTRY AND THE IMPLICATIONS OF CONSOLIDATION"

Good morning Chairman Rockefeller, Ranking Member Hutchison, and members of the committee.

Thank you for the opportunity to discuss the benefits and answer any questions related to the planned merger of equals between Continental Airlines and United Airlines that we announced on May 3. As we said at the time, this transaction will enable us to provide enhanced long-term career prospects for our more than 87,000 employees and superior service to our customers, especially those in small communities throughout the United States. Our combined company will be well-positioned to succeed in an increasingly competitive global and domestic aviation industry   better positioned than either airline would be standing alone or as alliance partners.

This merger will provide consumers access to 350 destinations in 59 countries around the world. We will offer a comprehensive network in the United States, and we will have strategically located international gateways to Asia, Europe, Latin America, the Middle East and Canada from well-placed domestic hubs throughout the country. We will have 10 hubs, eight in the continental U.S. (Chicago, Cleveland, Denver, Houston, Los Angeles, New York/Newark, San Francisco and Washington Dulles) and two others in Guam and in Tokyo. We will continue to provide service to all of the communities that our companies serve today.

This merger comes at a critical juncture for the U.S. aviation industry, which has confronted extremely difficult business challenges for the last decade. During this time, our industry has lost over 150,000 jobs, and there have been nearly 40 bankruptcies since 2001. U.S. airlines have lost a total of $60 billion since 2001.

While the economy and our industry are beginning to slowly recover from the worldwide recession, we continue to be subject to the volatility of fuel prices and an intensely competitive environment in all of our markets.

As individual companies, we have taken significant steps to respond to these challenges. United went through a bankruptcy restructuring and both airlines have become more efficient and reduced our cost structures. But to survive, we have also been forced to reduce the number of aircraft we fly, the number of destinations we serve and the number of people we employ.

At the same time, we have made significant operational improvements. United now ranks as the leading U.S. global airline in on-time performance as measured by the Department of Transportation, and Continental is regularly recognized in independent surveys for the high quality of its customer service. Through our joint venture and alliance relationships, we have provided enhanced benefits to our customers and achieved substantial synergies.

While we are proud of these recent improvements at our companies, we believe it is clearly in the best interests of our customers, employees, shareholders and the communities we serve to bring our two airlines together in a merger. This merger will provide a platform to build a more financially stable airline that can invest in our product and our people to succeed in a highly competitive environment and be better able to withstand future economic downturns and challenges. The fact is that sustained profitability is the only way to improve service and reward employees over the long term.

The Merger Will Benefit Customers

By bringing together two of the most complementary route networks of any U.S. carriers, the merger of Continental and United will give travelers expanded access to an unparalleled global network. It combines United's Midwest, West Coast and Pacific in New York/New Jersey, theroutes with East Coast, the South, Latin America and across the Atlantic.

Customers will have access to 116 new domestic destinations; 40 will be new to United customers, and 76 will be new to Continental customers. The merger will create more than 1,000 new domestic connecting city pairs served by the combined carrier, providing additional convenience to customers.

Our fully optimized fleets and routes will provide greater flexibility, options, connectivity and convenience for customers. This improved connectivity and direct service options, as well as improved service, are expected to enable the combined airline to generate $800-$900 million in annual revenue synergies and these synergies are not dependent on fare increases.

Importantly, the combined airline will be better able to enhance the travel experience for our customers through investments in technology, the acquisition of new planes and the implementation of the best practices of both airlines. The new airline will be more cost effective; we expect to realize cost-savings synergies of $200-$300 million per year, mostly through reductions in overhead such as rationalizing our two information technology platforms, combining facilities and corporate functions such as finance, marketing, sales and advertising.

We will have one of the youngest and most fuel-efficient fleets among the major U.S. network carriers, as well as the flexibility to manage our fleet more effectively. With one of the best new aircraft order books in the industry, we will also be able to retire older, less efficient aircraft. This will result not only in greater efficiency but less environmental impact from our fleet.

Once the merger is complete, customers will also participate in the program, which will give millions of members more opportunities to earn and redeem miles than ever before. Through Star Alliance, the leading global alliance network, our customers will also continue to benefit from service to more than 1,000 destinations worldwide.

The Merger Provides Job Stability for Employees

The past decade has been a tumultuous time for our employees. They have faced ongoing uncertainty as the industry has been forced to shed tens of thousands of jobs. In fact, in January 2009, the full time equivalent employees for the U.S. airline industry numbered 390,700   that figure is 151,000   or more than 25 percent   less than the all time high airline employment figure of 542,300. Employees have been forced to weather the volatility of oil prices and the challenges of terrorist attacks, increased security, a massive recession and unforeseen events such as SARS, H1N1 and volcanic ash. Through all of this, they have continued to perform at their best, providing our customers with clean, safe and reliable air travel.

We're proud of the employees do every day. The merger will offer our employees improvedwork that our long-term career opportunities and enhanced job stability by being part of a larger, financially stronger and more geographically diverse carrier that is better able to compete successfully in the global marketplace and withstand the volatility of our industry.

We will continue to serve all of the communities that we serve today and we expect that any necessary reductions in front line employees will come from retirements, normal attrition and voluntary programs. Our plan is to integrate our workforces in a fair and equitable way. Our focus will be on creating cooperative labor relations, including negotiating contracts with our collective bargaining units that are fair to the company and fair to our employees. United has two members of its collective bargaining units on its Board of Directors, and the seats allocated to the collective bargaining units will continue to be part of the Board of the combined company.

The merged company's headquarters go. In Houston, we will continue to have a significantwill be in Chica presence and will remain one of Houston's largest private . Houston will be our largest hub andemployers will continue be a premier gateway to Latin America for more travelers than ever before. Some corporate positions will remain in Houston and our CEO will have an office there as well as in Chicago. Over time, as our business grows as a result of the merger, we expect to see a net gain in jobs in Houston.

We expect to adopt the best aspects of each company's culture . People at bothand practices companies have come to know, admire and learn from their counterparts in many functions due to our joint venture and Star Alliance relationships, and we are confident that we can integrate our organizations fairly, effectively, and efficiently.

Service to Small Communities Will Be Enhanced

As network carriers, we have a long history of serving small- and medium-sized communities. United is proud to fly passengers from places like Portland, Maine to Honolulu or Charleston, South Carolina to Chicago, while Continental's service to and from Houston has been instrumental to the growth of the 20 Texas communities served.

Air travel opens up the world and provides business and leisure opportunities to all Americans, no matter where they live. Airlines are often the lifeblood of small communities, not only because of the economic benefits they provide, but due to their civic and charitable contributions and the volunteer activities of their employees. Both of our companies are committed community partners with robust corporate contributions and responsibility programs and we strongly support

The turmoil in our industry has been devastating to many small- and medium-sized communities. Since 2000, more than 100 small communities have lost all network carrier service. Approximately 50 more have seen their service levels cut, losing at least half of their seats.

CHART ONE
THE MERGER MAKES A MORE EFFICIENT CARRIER, BETTER ABLE TO SERVE SMALL COMMUNITIES

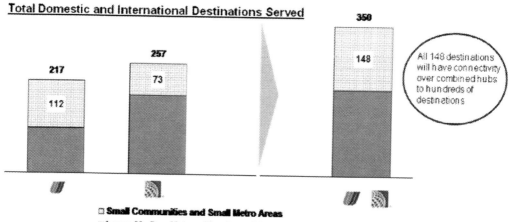

Total Domestic and International Destinations Served

□ Small Communities and Small Metro Areas
■ Large, Medium Metropolitan Areas & International Destinations

Source: OAG FY 2010.
Notes: Consolidated operations. Domestic destinations with at least one route served 20 times by either United or Continental during at least one month in 2010. International destinations with at least one route served 12 times by either United or Continental during at least one month in 2010. Bristol, UK is excluded for Continental as it will be cancelled in November. Moses Lake, WA and Oxnard, CA are excluded for United as they will be cancelled in June. Airports in the following major metropolitan areas are grouped: New York (JFK, LGA, EWR), Washington (DCA, IAD, BWI), San Francisco (SFO, OAK), Chicago (ORD, MDW), Houston (IAH, HOU), Dallas (DFW, DAL), Los Angeles (LAX, BUR, LGB) Cleveland (CLE, CAK), Tampa (TPA, PIE), Cincinnati (CVG, DAY), and Miami (MIA, FLL). In addition, the following small community airports are also not counted as separate destinations because they are adjacent to a larger airport - Bedford, MA; Carlsbad, CA; Houston/Ellington Field, TX; Mesa, AZ; Seattle/Boeing Field, WA; Wilmington, DE. Airports in major international cities are grouped.

Low cost carriers have not filled this void because service to these communities is typically inconsistent with their business model. They are more-often dependent on point-to-point, high-density routes and often have one-size aircraft, which makes it difficult for them to serve these small communities. As a result, approximately 200 of these small communities and metropolitan areas, many of which have fewer than 500 passengers traveling to or from their airports daily, are served only by network carriers.

When we announced our merger, we committed to continuing to provide service to all of the communities our airlines currently serve, including 148 small communities and metropolitan areas **(CHART ONE).** This service enables residents of small communities to connect through our eight mainland domestic hubs and travel on to hundreds of destinations on thousands of routes worldwide. The combined airline will offer these travelers access to 350 destinations in 59 countries.

Following the merger, 93 of the 116 destinations that would be new to either Continental or United passengers would be small communities. As a result, a businessperson will be able to fly from Tyler, Texas to Sydney, Australia on a single airline.

The Merger Will Enhance Competition

The potential impact of this merger must be viewed in light of the fundamental changes that have occurred in our industry since 2000. The increased competition from low cost carriers (LCCs) has been dramatic as they have experienced tremendous growth over the past decade. They operate profitably at lower unit revenues than traditional network airlines, generally due to significant cost advantages related to their less costly point-to-point business model. Consequently, their presence limits the ability of their competitors to increase fares.

CHART TWO
U.S. DOMESTIC PASSENGER SHARE: MERGED AIRLINE WILL BE ONLY
THIRD LARGEST WITH 16%

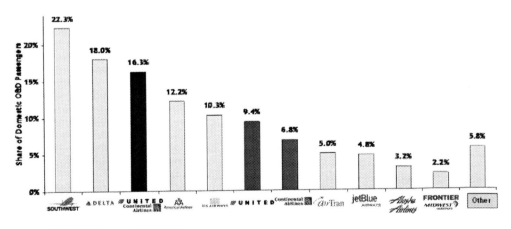

Source: U.S. DOT O&D Survey YE 2009 Q3.
Note: Frontier includes Midwest. Share of domestic O&D passengers. Largest Other carriers include Hawaiian (1.6%), Allegiant (1.2%), Spirit (1.1%), Virgin America (0.9%), and Sun Country (0.3%).

Industry-wide, LCCs now compete for 80% of all domestic travelers. In fact, Southwest has grown to become the largest domestic airline in the U.S., in terms of passengers and will continue in that position after our merger **(CHART TWO).** Over 85% of passengers traveling non-stop on either Continental or United have an LCC alternative. LCCs compete on domestic city-pairs accounting for 77% of United and Continental's combined , and 46 of each of Continental passengers top 50 routes, have LCCand United's competition.

There once was an assumption that LCCs would have difficulty competing at the hubs of network carriers. This assumption has long since been disproven. LCCs directly compete at all of our hub airports and have very large presences at airports adjacent to our hubs, such as Hobby in Houston, Akron near Cleveland, BWI near Washington and Midway in Chicago. LCCs have market shares in our hub cities ranging from 28% in Cleveland to 50% in Denver and San Francisco.

LCCs are increasingly being used by business travelers and are targeting those travelers by providing amenities such as preferred seating and boarding access. They are also providing service from the United States to international destinations, including Mexico, the Caribbean, Latin America and Canada.

In addition to the growth of LCCs, competition from international carriers has increased. Mergers between Air France and KLM; Lufthansa, SWISS, bmi, Brussels Airlines and Austrian; British Airways and Iberia; and Cathay Pacific and Hong Kong Dragon Airlines have given these preeminent global carriers international networks and global reach that overshadow those of U.S. network carriers. In 2000, the top two airlines in terms of worldwide revenue, American Airlines and United, were both U.S.-based. Today, the top two are Lufthansa and Air France/KLM **(CHART THREE)**. In fact, more than half of all transatlantic capacity and more than two-thirds of all transpacific capacity is provided by foreign carriers. The merged carrier will be able to compete far more effectively with foreign carriers and to maintain competitive domestic service to cities large and small in the U.S.

CHART THREE
U.S. NETWORK CARRIERS HAVE LOST THEIR #1 AND #2 WORLDWIDE REVENUE RANKINGS

Top 10 Carriers Ranked by Revenue

	CY2000				CY2009	
Rank	Airline	Operating Revenue ($B)		Rank	Airline	Operating Revenue ($B)
1	American	$19.7		1	Lufthansa	$31.0
2	United	$19.4		2	Air France-KLM	$29.2
3	Delta	$16.7		3	Delta/NW	$28.1
4	JAL	$15.4		4	American	$19.9
5	Lufthansa	$14.0		5	JAL	$16.4
6	British Airways	$13.7		6	United	$16.3
7	ANA	$11.5		7	ANA	$12.9
8	Northwest	$11.4		8	British Airways	$12.6
9	Air France	$11.1		9	Continental	$12.6
10	Continental	$9.9		10	Emirates*	$11.2

* Emirates 2009 is full year ending June 2009.
Source: For 2000 – Airline Business September 2001. For 2009: Domestic Carriers Company 10-Ks. Foreign Carriers Press releases and Annual Reports.
Notes: 2009 foreign carriers' operating revenues are calculated using the following exchange rates for 2009: 1USD=0.719055EUR; 1USD=0.641005GBP; 1USD=93.53617JPY; 1USD=3.67291AED.

Additionally, well-funded newcomers (such as Emirates and Jet Airways) are making inroads into U.S. international routes from emerging economies in the Middle East and South

Asia. This trend will continue, and is a credit to the success of the Open Skies policy as these agreements expose U.S. carriers to more competition than ever before.

Price competition in our industry has also increased due to the ready availability and transparency of fare information to consumers through online sites such as Expedia and Orbitz. Consumers have become more savvy and sophisticated as they search for the fare that meets g airfarestheir needs. like raising the price of milk...the internet can hunt has some empty seats to fill, it will have to cut the price because getting something for that seat is better than flying (Scott McCartney, "As Airlines it empty" *Wall Street Journal* Cut   ,
Who 6/5/08). Online sites have expanded their business models and now offer targeted services to corporations and business travelers.

In short, the changing dynamics of the airline industry have resulted in robust competition that maintains significant downward pressure on fares. As a result, airfare prices have declined by more than 30 percent over the last decade on an inflation adjusted basis **(CHART FOUR)**.

Especially given this landscape and the relative ease with which LCCs can enter into competition with network carriers and other LCCs, this merger will not result in a reduction in competition. There are only 15 overlapping non-stop domestic routes among the hundreds that we fly (and no overlapping international routes). The combined carrier's any individual overlapping route isability to constrained because each has current non-stop competitors. Moreover, extensive competitive connecting service further constrains pricing.

CHART FOUR
DESPITE NUMEROUS MERGERS, AVERAGE PRICE* CONTINUES TO DECLINE

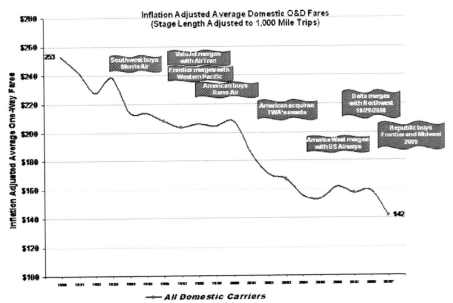

Sources: US DOT O&D Survey. CPI from U.S. Bureau of Labor Statistics.
Notes: 2009 Dollars. 2009 FYE Q3.
*Average price per passenger based on average price per mile then adjusted to 1,000 mile trips.

CHART FIVE
NON-STOP OVERLAPS

	City-Pair	Non-Stop Competitors	Current LCC Non-Stop Competitors	UA/CO O&D Passenger Share (%)	LCC O&D Passenger Share (%)
	Hubs				
1	Washington - Houston	3	Southwest	62.6%	27.0%
2	Los Angeles - Houston*	3	Southwest	54.6%	35.8%
3	Houston - San Francisco	3	Southwest	57.5%	35.4%
4	Denver - Cleveland	3	Frontier	46.0%	48.7%
5	Chicago - Houston	4	Southwest	53.4%	33.3%
6	Denver - Houston	4	Southwest and Frontier	60.4%	38.3%
7	Chicago - Cleveland	4	Southwest	40.8%	47.6%
8	Washington - Cleveland	4	Southwest	40.4%	53.0%
9	Denver - New York	5	Frontier and jetBlue	62.7%	26.1%
10	Los Angeles - New York	6	jetBlue and Virgin America	24.3%	36.0%
11	Chicago - New York	6	Southwest and jetBlue	42.0%	9.1%**
12	New York - San Francisco	6	jetBlue and Virgin America	37.2%	32.5%
13	Washington - New York	7	Southwest and jetBlue	18.6%	10.2%
	Non-Hub-to-Hub				
14	Los Angeles - Kahului	4	—	52.0%	—
15	Los Angeles - Honolulu	5	—	29.6%	—

*Reflects recently announced new service by United from LAX–IAH starting Aug 24.
** Does not fully reflect Southwest LGA-MDW service that began June 29, 2009. LCC share for Q3–Q4 2009 is 13.3%.
Source: OAG May 2010; U.S. DOT O&D Survey YE 2009 Q3.
Notes: Consolidated operations. Competitors with at least 5 roundtrips per week. Delta includes Northwest. Frontier includes Midwest. Airports in the following metropolitan areas are grouped: Chicago (ORD, MDW), Cincinnati (CVG, DAY), Cleveland (CLE, CAK), Dallas (DFW, DAL), Houston (HOU, IAH), Los Angeles (LAX, BUR, LGB), Miami (MIA, FLL), New York (LGA, JFK, EWR), San Francisco (SFO, OAK), Washington DC (DCA, IAD, BWI), and Tampa (TPA, PIE).

On each of these 15 non-stop overlapping routes, after the merger, travelers would be served by at least one other carrier, but more often two, three, four or five. All but two of the overlapping routes are served by an LCC and six are served by two LCCs **(CHART FIVE)**.

The Merger is a Natural Extension of Our Current Relationship

About two years ago, our companies began an extensive alliance relationship. We are both members of Star Alliance, the leading global alliance network. Domestically, we have a codeshare arrangement, frequent flyer reciprocity and shared lounge access.

We have antitrust immunity for international coordination including our A++ transatlantic joint venture that also includes Air Canada and Lufthansa. We have an immunity application pending with ANA that includes a transpacific joint venture, in connection with the Open Skies agreement initialed and soon to be implemented with Japan.

While these agreements have generated significant synergies and customer benefits, they do not provide the cost savings and employee and customer benefits of a merger. For example, following a merger, we can fully optimize our schedules and integrate our fleets. Our combined mainline fleet of more than 700 aircraft of a broad range of sizes and mission capabilities will enable the most efficient utilization of seat capacity. We will be able to reassign aircraft across the network to better meet demand on different routes, yielding a net increase in annual passengers and improving the business mix of those passengers through the appeal of our broad combined network.

The merger will also enhance our frequent flyer programs. Currently, it is sometimes difficult to obtain reciprocal benefits, elite recognition and awards. A combined program would offer more benefit to customers as they accrue and redeem awards across our combined network on a seamless frequent flyer program.

Our alliance relationship has given each airline the opportunity to know and partially integrate the systems, practices and procedures of the other. As a result, it gives us great confidence that we can successfully integrate our two companies once the merger closes.

CONCLUSION

Each of our companies has a long and proud history of independence. Continental and United are among the pioneers in the aviation industry and, in fact, have the same founder, Walter T. Varney.

Although our companies have been performing better since the economic recovery began, we analyzed the competitive environment and reflected on the volatility that has plagued our industry. As we looked ahead, we each strongly believed that our combined future was brighter than our standalone future, that this is the right time for a merger, and that we have found the right merger partner.

As we have talked to our customers, our employees and our shareholders, we have felt a great sense of excitement about this merger. By bringing the best of both organizations together, we believe we can not only create a world-class airline with enduring strengths, but also serve our customers and communities better than ever, provide security and stability for our employees and benefit shareholders with a strong financial foundation.

We look forward to continuing to outline the benefits of this merger in Washington, D.C., and throughout the country and the rest of the world. But more importantly, we look forward to our people working together to create the world's leading airline.

In: Airline Industry Mergers: Background and Issues
Editor: Felix J. Mercado

ISBN: 978-1-61761-993-9
© 2011 Nova Science Publishers, Inc.

Chapter 5

Testimony of Robert Roach, Jr., General Vice President, before the Committee on Commerce, Science & Transportation, Hearing on "The Financial State of the Airline Industry and the Implications of Consolidation"

Thank you, Chairman Rockefeller, Ranking Member Hutchison and members of this Committee for the opportunity to speak to you today. My name is Robert Roach, Jr., General Vice President of the International Association of Machinists and Aerospace Workers (IAM), the largest airline union in North America, which recently entered into an alliance with the Japan Federation of Aviation Workers' Unions (KOHKUREN). In my capacity as a member of the Executive Board and Management Committee of the International Transport Workers' Federation (ITF), I had the ITF review my prepared testimony and they have given their authorization for me to speak on their behalf. My comments today are not only on behalf of the 720,000 members of the Machinists Union, but also reflect the position of 4.6 million ITF members.

The Machinists Union represents United Airlines and/or Continental Airlines workers in the flight attendant; ramp; customer service; reservation agent; fleet technical instructor; maintenance instructor; security guard; and food service employee classifications, plus customer service agents at United's frequent-flier subsidiary, Mileage Plus, Inc. The IAM also represents flight attendants at Continental's wholly-owned subsidiary Continental Micronesia and flight attendants at Continental and United regional partner ExpressJet Airlines. In total, the IAM represents more than 26,000 workers who will be affected by this proposed merger. Our bargaining relationship with each airline spans many decades.

PERPETUAL CRISIS

The airline industry has been in continuous turmoil since the passage of deregulation in 1978. Merger proponents complain about overcapacity as a major reason for industry consolidation, but mergers will not address overcapacity. Braniff, Eastern, Pan Am, TWA, Northwest Airlines, People Express, Aloha Airlines and others have all disappeared from the industry landscape, but the problem of overcapacity remains.

We cannot look at the United-Continental transaction in isolation. As the Delta-Northwest merger moves toward its completion, the United-Continental merger takes center stage. Waiting in the wings is a possible third merger, perhaps between US Airways and American Airlines, each a product of recent consolidation with America West and TWA, respectively. We agree with House Transportation and Infrastructure Committee Chairman James Oberstar when he wrote the Department of Justice stating, "This merger will move the country far down the path of an airline system dominated by three mega-carriers...If United and Continental merge, another domino in a chain of mergers will fall, and there will be strong pressure for further consolidation[1]."

Does anyone really believe that having only a few major airlines in operation, each with immense market control and offering consumers fewer choices, will benefit the country? If one of these mega-carriers should fail, how would that impact the country?

The Machinists Union has serious concerns not only about the viability of a combined United/Continental carrier, but also for the long-term sustainability of each carrier independently. In fact, our concern is for the entire industry, and we do not believe mergers alone provide the answers. Congress has spent a considerable amount of time debating the issue of entities that are too big to be allowed to fail. Our concern is we are creating airlines that are too big to succeed.

I am not advocating that we maintain the status quo in the airline industry. When there are problems, we must seek solutions. But perhaps we should take a step back and not rush to judgment or consolidation. It is time we seek a new vision for the future of air transportation in the United States.

It was clear to the Machinists Union in 1993 that deregulation had failed. The Clinton administration recognized the problems facing the air transportation industry and empanelled the National Commission to Ensure a Strong Competitive Airline Industry. One of my predecessors, IAM General Vice President John Peterpaul, served on the Commission. The Commissioners were charged with investigating and devising recommendations that would resolve the crisis in the industry and return it to financial health and stability.

The Committee essentially recommended no substantial regulatory changes and believed that market forces would stabilize the industry. The IAM's representative on the Commission was the only dissenter, arguing that deregulation destabilized the industry and government intervention was necessary.

This country needs the major airlines, or so-called legacy carriers. While low-cost carriers fill an important niche, the air transportation system would collapse without traditional hub-and-spoke carriers. If you want to fly to Europe, Asia, South America or the Middle East you will be flying one of the legacy carriers, or another nation's airline. As John Peterpaul said, "Hubs serve as collection and distribution centers for air traffic, making it possible to serve many more communities than would be feasible with simple linear, point-to point service."[2] It is a mistake to think that as legacy airlines merge and hubs are eliminated that start-ups or low-cost carriers are capable of filling the void.

The Machinists Union's assertion that deregulation had failed to deliver on its promises was ignored in 1993 in favor of supporting airline industry executives who advocated staying the course. Congress now has another chance to make effective changes to this industry.

United and US Airways' pension terminations alone have cost the Pension Benefit Guaranty Board (PBGC) $10 billion and beneficiaries $5 billion[3]. Inflation-adjusted salaries for airline employees have grown less than 5% since 1979[3]. There have been 162 airline bankruptcy filings since 1978[4], with bankruptcies accelerating in the last decade, including the liquidations of Aloha Airlines, ATA and Midway Airlines. Since 1978, 150 low-cost carriers began operations, with less than a dozen still providing service today.[4] More than 100 communities have lost *all* commercial air service in the last 10 years.[4] The industry has lost more than $60 billion in the last decade, and 163,000 industry jobs have disappeared since 2001.[5]

The so-called low-cost airlines are not immune to the industry's problems and are also looking for additional consolidation to help them survive. For example, US Airways, which became a low-cost carrier after two bankruptcies and a merger with America West Airlines, is now aggressively seeking a merger partner. "Further down the road there's a high probability that US Airways will wind up merging with either United, Delta or American," said US Airways President Scott Kirby.[6]

Even Alfred Kahn, the major architect of deregulation, has said, "I must concede that the industry has demonstrated a more severe and chronic susceptibility to destructive competition than I, along with the other enthusiastic proponents of deregulation, was prepared to concede or predict."[7]

This industry is crying out for limited re-regulation.

Deregulation in this industry – and others –has had disastrous effects. Left completely to their own devices, corporations put their profits first without regard to the impact it has on the nation.

The 2007 financial and housing meltdown was a result of unregulated corporate greed in the banking and mortgage industries. Instead of only traditional banks offering mortgages, non-banks were allowed to enter the mortgage market. Predatory lenders aggressively targeted unqualified borrowers. Investment banks sold mortgage packages to Wall Street – all largely unregulated. When the mortgages defaulted – because many should never have been made in the first place – Wall Street collapsed, and took the rest of the economy with it.

One only has to look at the news this evening to see the toxic results of energy industry deregulation suffocating our Gulf shores. Local fishing and tourism industries are being destroyed, not to mention the cataclysmic environmental impact. Oversight and enforcement of BP's operations were woefully inadequate, in spite of a decade of documented safety violations at BP locations across the United States.[8]

Some industries are too critical to the United States to be allowed to regulate themselves. The airline industry needs to be stabilized because it drives $1 .4 trillion in economic activity and contributes $692 billion per year to the Gross Domestic Product (GDP).[9] It is too vital to the nation's commerce to be ignored, taken for granted or left to its own destructive ways.

Today, Congress is considering increased oversight of both the financial and oil industries to provide more regulation. Such action is necessary and long overdue, but it took catastrophes to prompt action. There have been three decades worth of evidence that airline deregulation has failed. At what point do we take another look at this beleaguered airline industry? We need to be forward-thinking before we are asked to bailout the airline industry – again.

It is clear that airline deregulation has failed to deliver on its promises of a stable and profitable industry, and staying the course will continue the industry's downward spiral. Airline bankruptcies will continue, more proud airlines will disappear, employees will continue to suffer and passengers will receive less service. Albert Einstein said, "Insanity is doing the same thing over and over again and expecting a different result."

We can close our eyes and believe that repeating the same mistake for thirty years will eventually bring different results, or we can effect real change and have an efficient and competitive air transportation industry.

I do not propose a complete return to the days of the Civil Aeronautics Board and complete re-regulation, but some additional form of government involvement is necessary.

Although I do not agree with everything former American Airlines CEO Robert Crandall says about the airline industry, I share his opinion that, "market–based approaches alone have not and will not produce the aviation system our country needs" and that "some form of government intervention is required."[10]

The IAM believes fares need to be regulated. We must have fare minimums, because if an airline is allowed to charge less for a ticket than it costs to provide the service, we will have more airline bankruptcies and further consolidation until we have only a single airline left in the United States.

Airline business plans today focus on lowering standards, eliminating services and reducing ticket prices to the bone to put competitors out of business, making a profitable industry impossible. The GAO estimates that median ticket prices have dropped nearly 40% since 1980, although the costs of aircraft, airport leases and fuel have increased dramatically.[11] Employees have been subsidizing the low ticket prices. No business can survive if they sell their product for less than what it costs to deliver their goods.

The long-term cost of under pricing tickets is too extreme. Pan Am, TWA, Eastern, Northwest and Aloha Airlines all survived for more than half a century, but could not endure the insanity of cutting prices to eliminate the competition.

MERGER SCRUTINY

Although we have met with United and Continental both separately and jointly, information has been slow in coming. The Machinists Union and our 26,000 members at the two airlines do not have enough details about the merger's impact on employees to determine if this merger would be in their best interests. The carriers admit that many of our most important issues, such as pensions, workforce integration, union representation, prevailing wages and working conditions will largely remain unresolved until after the Department of Justice rules on the merger. To the carriers' credit, they have agreed to a communication system through which we can obtain the information to address employee concerns, but that does not answer our questions today.

United Airlines has $8.5 billion in long-term debt[12], and Continental has $5.3 billion in long-term debt[13] – and they are considered healthy by industry standards. The merged entity would start out $13.8 billion in debt. What is their business plan to deal with the debt structure?

Merging airlines is much more difficult than just painting planes and combining websites. American Airlines' 2001 acquisition of TWA's assets resulted in tremendous job loss, employee integration problems and the closing of a hub in St. Louis, Missouri. The America West-US Airways merger cost the city of Pittsburgh, Pennsylvania its hub, and employee integration problems for some classifications persist five years after the merger. The 2008 Delta-Northwest merger is still far from being completed and managements' promises to preserve all front-line jobs in the merger were quickly broken.

With tens of thousands of employees from two different corporate cultures involved, jobs are inevitably lost in mergers and integrating employees groups is never as smooth as management claims. As with any service industry, employees upset with management provide an inferior product. How employees are treated in this merger will ultimately determine its fate. Southwest Airlines founder Herb Kelleher has said, "Happy and pleased employees take care of the customers. And happy customers take care of shareholders by coming back.[14]" An airline merger that does not take employees into consideration has the potential to take two viable carriers and create a combined airline destined to fail.

AIRLINE ALLIANCES

Several years ago, the IAM raised concerns with respect to airline alliances. In our opinion, these alliances served as a potential mechanism for allowing airlines a path around antitrust laws. Unfortunately, our concerns have been substantiated. In some cases, they have served as the foundation for airlines to consolidate their operations. Time and time again, consolidations are announced only after both airlines have operated in the same airline alliance structure.

Continental and United Airlines represent the latest consolidation of airlines in the same alliance. Continental's membership in the Star Alliance essentially started a merger on the installment plan. Given the prevalence of alliances here at home, what will alliances ultimately mean for the traveling public, particularly if they lead to further consolidation and route frequencies are cut, if not altogether abandoned?

The implications for worldwide air travel are even more profound, particularly for U.S. consumers. Given the rapid acceleration of outsourcing of most job classifications, will alliances result in the outsourcing of most domestic work on carriers to workers at airlines in other countries? We have already seen thousands of U.S. aviation jobs shifted to countries like China, Singapore, and the Philippines as U.S. air carriers outsource call centers and maintenance work. Given the lack of proper oversight by the FAA, as well as inadequate quality control mechanisms, this development should raise alarms for any policymaker that sees domestic job security and consumer interests a priority.

EFFECTS OF THE MERGER ON HUBS

The effects of a Continental/United merger would be felt most resoundingly in the upper Midwest and Mid-Atlantic states. The new carrier would most likely eliminate or downsize at least two of its hubs, in Cleveland, OH (CLE) and Washington-Dulles (IAD) in order to remove excess capacity. Closing hubs initiates a cascade of job loss that begins with airline employees and continues throughout the community to firms that provide services to the airline.

In the Midwest, United's leadership position at Chicago-O'Hare (ORD) could mean the elimination of Continental's CLE hub operation. CLE is only 307 miles from ORD. Continental's CLE hub is the smallest of their three hubs and has just recently started to grow again following post 9/11 downsizing. United is Chicago's hometown airline with unparalleled facilities and routes from ORD. CLE and the northern Ohio area have already been suffering greatly from the economic downturn and the mortgage crisis, and eliminating a major local employer would have drastic effects on the local economy.

Such a move would dramatically affect air service for the northern Ohio area, for which CLE serves as the closest major hub. Large corporations with their headquarters in CLE, such as National City Corporation, American Greetings, Eaton, Forest City Enterprises, Sherwin-Williams Paints, Key Bank and Progressive Auto Insurance would lose access to direct domestic and international flights. Communities through Michigan, Kentucky, Tennessee, Ohio, Illinois, Wisconsin, and other states would lose their regional jet service operated by Continental Express, in many cases leaving them only with one airline alternative.

A different situation exists in the Northeast, where United's smaller IAD hub is only 215 miles from Continental's EWR "Global Gateway." EWR is Continental's primary international hub with nonstop service to nearly 1 00 destinations outside the United States. IAD serves as United's primary gateway to Europe, but its size and scope is nowhere near matching Continental's EWR operation.

Due to the large size of the local Washington, D.C. market, it is presumed that instead of a full-fledged hub closure, IAD would be downsized into a much smaller hub or a large focus city. IAD benefits from the fact that there is a perimeter restriction on flights from nearby Reagan National Airport (DCA) to destinations more than 1,500 miles away, which requires most flights to the West Coast to be operated out of IAD.

A Continental/United combination would also concentrate competition at many non-hub airports. They would be the largest carrier at Boston Logan (BOS), number 3 at New Your-LaGuardia (LGA), number 4 at New York–Kennedy (JFK), and the second largest carrier in Honolulu, Hawaii (HNL) after Hawaiian Airlines. At all of these airports it would be necessary to combine personnel and facilities, which would most likely result in layoffs.

We have to ask ourselves if the merging of these carriers and wholesale reshaping of the industry will destroy competition and harm consumers on routes throughout the United States.

As details about the combined carriers' business plan emerge, it must be closely scrutinized to determine if a merger will result in a successful entity or not. We ask Congress to help us determine if this transaction will be good for employees and consumers.

PENSIONS

The Machinists Union is concerned that employees could lose defined benefit pension plans as a result of the merger. Continental ramp service, stock clerks and public contact employees all participate in a Continental company-sponsored single-employer defined benefit pension plan, while their IAM-represented counterparts at United participate in the multi-employer IAM National Pension Plan (NPP). Continental's IAMrepresented flight attendants also participate in one of Continental's defined benefit pension plans and have negotiated the IAM NPP as a contingency plan. United flight attendants do not currently have a defined benefit pension plan, and the Pension Benefit Guaranty Corporation (PBGC) has prohibited United from sponsoring a single- employer pension plan.

The IAM believes that all employees deserve defined benefit pension plans. The carriers acknowledged that harmonizing pensions would be a complex issue, and although they have given it much thought, they did not know how it would be resolved.

In spite of United abandoning its pension obligations in bankruptcy, the IAM fought hard and ensured our members would have a replacement defined benefit plan. Just as we did in United's bankruptcy, the IAM will not allow our members' retirement security to become a causality of this merger.

COLLECTIVE BARGAINING

The Machinists Union is currently in contract negotiations for all eight classifications where we have members at the two carriers - seven at United plus Continental flight attendants. United negotiations have been ongoing for more than a year, and bargaining with Continental began late in 2009.

Regulatory and shareholder approval are far from certain at this point, and the Machinists Union is committed to negotiating new agreements to cover our members at each airline. It is premature for anyone to talk about combining the carriers' employees, and each airline must recognize their responsibility to continue bargaining in good faith.

SENIORITY

Seniority integration is always a major concern in mergers. Although airlines often promise fair and equitable integration of seniority, fair and equitable is a very subjective term and should not be left up to the carriers to decide. Some past mergers have resulted in employees losing decades of seniority – I am one of them. My seniority date was changed from 1975 to 2001 after American Airlines purchased TWA's assets in bankruptcy.

Continental Airlines is the product of many past mergers in the wake of deregulation, and in some cases seniority was integrated unilaterally by the then Frank Lorenzo-led carrier. The Machinists will ensure seniority is protected in this merger, but again, this is an issue to be addressed after representation issues are resolved. At the IAM's insistence, both airlines have agreed not to engage in workgroup integration discussions until representation issues are resolved.

HISTORY OF SACRIFICE

United Airlines employees have suffered greatly through the carrier's bankruptcy, the longest and most expensive airline bankruptcy in history.

Immediately after its Chapter 11 filing, United Airlines asked a bankruptcy judge to impose 14% "emergency" pay cuts on IAM members. More long-term cuts in pay and benefits cost IAM members $460 million a year (or $2.644 billion over the life of the agreement). United then took steps to cut health benefits for existing retirees and filed a motion in court to ask a judge to impose further cuts if agreements could not be reached with the retirees' representatives

In the summer of 2004 United ceased funding its pension plans, the first in a series of steps which ultimately led to the termination of its company-sponsored pension plans.

In January 2005, United once again sought and received "emergency" pay cuts from the bankruptcy court - this time it was 11%. Six months later IAM members gave up another $176 million a year to save United. Savings attributable to the termination of IAM member's pensions saved United an additional $217 million a year.

In total, IAM members were forced to sacrifice more than *$4.6 billion* for United Airlines. United employees have been subsidizing the airline since 2003, and each day without a new contract that sacrifice continues.

Continental Airlines' employees also sacrificed more the $500 million a year to keep their airline out of bankruptcy during their last round of collective bargaining.

So, employees have the right to question the motives behind this merger and fear they would be forced to subsidize it.

CONCLUSION

The business plan for the proposed airline must receive close scrutiny. The IAM is concerned that the new entity may be too big to succeed without some form of industry re-regulation, and failure of such a large entity could be disastrous to employees, the industry and the general economy.

As this merger proposal moves forward, the Machinists Union asks regulators to take the merger's impact on employees into consideration. A combined carrier must offer employees more stability and opportunity than are available at the two independent airlines. The merger cannot be at the expense of workers who have already sacrificed to keep their airlines aloft. United and Continental employees did not accept job cuts and wages and benefit changes when their employers restructured just to lose out again in a merger.

The Machinists Union believes that airline mergers should have conditions, including requirements that protect employees, consumers and taxpayers – all of whom have been hurt by this unregulated industry. Employees must have their jobs, wages, benefits and pensions protected. If the architects of a merger can guarantee themselves bonuses and lucrative severance packages, then they can do the same for front-line employees. All cities that the airlines currently serve, not just profitable ones, must continue to be served. Pension obligations should be upheld in mergers, and consolidation should not be a vehicle for airlines to dump their pensions on the PBGC.

United and Continental would not be seeking to merge today if employees had not stepped up to save them in the past. United and Continental need to demonstrate how the proposed merger would benefit employees, consumers, and the cities and states the airlines currently serve.

Thank you again for the opportunity to speak with you today. The Machinists Union recognizes it is in the nation's interest to have a safe, reliable, competitive and profitable air transportation industry. We are committed to working with Congress, the Departments of Justice and Transportation, and the air carriers to achieve that goal.

I look forward to your questions.

End Notes

[1] Chairman James Oberstar's letter to the Department of Justice, May 5, 2010

[2] *Dissenting Opinion*, by Commissioner John Peterpaul to the Report of the National Commission to Ensure a Strong Competitive Airline Industry, August 19, 1993

[3] *Airline Deregulation*, United States Government Accountability Office Report GAO-06-630, June 2006

[4] *Flying Blind*, Dēmos, 2009

[5] Testimony by ATA President and CEO Jim May Before House Appropriations Subcommittee on Transportation, Housing, Urban Development and Related Agencies on Aviation Stakeholder Priorities for Maintaining a Safe and Viable Aviation System, March 18, 2010

[6] *US Airways: Merger Probability Is High,* by Ted Reed, TheStreet.com, June 1, 2010 http://www.thestreet.com/story/10771279/1/us-airways

[7] *Change, Challenge, and Competition: A Review of the Airline Commission Report",* by Alfred E. Kahn, 1993

[8] *Reports at BP Over Years Find History of Problems*, By Abrahm Lustgarten and Ryan Knutson. Washington Post, June 8, 2010

[9] *The World Airline Report*, Air Transport World, June 1, 2009 http://atwonline.com/eco-aviation/article/world-airline-report-0309

[10] *Charge More, Merge Less, Fly Better,* by Robert Crandall, The New York Times OP-ED, April 21, 2008

[11] *Airline Deregulation*, United States Government Accountability Office Report GAO-06-630, June 2006

[12] Continental Airlines 10-K filing with the Securities and Exchange Commission, filed 2/17/10.

[13] United Airlines 10-K filing with the Securities and Exchange Commission, filed 2/26/2010.

[14] *From the Corner Office - Herb Kelleher*, by Mary Vinnedge, Retrieved from success.com on May 26, 2010, http://www.successmagazine.com/From-the-Corner-Office-Herb-Kelleher/PARAMS/article/390/channel/19

In: Airline Industry Mergers: Background and Issues
Editor: Felix J. Mercado

ISBN: 978-1-61761-993-9
© 2011 Nova Science Publishers, Inc.

Chapter 6

TESTIMONY OF CHARLES LEOCHA, DIRECTOR, CONSUMER TRAVEL ALLIANCE, BEFORE THE COMMITTEE ON COMMERCE, SCIENCE & TRANSPORTATION, HEARING ON "THE FINANCIAL STATE OF THE AIRLINE INDUSTRY AND THE IMPLICATIONS OF CONSOLIDATION"

Thank you, Chairman Rockefeller for giving passengers a seat at this congressional table and an opportunity to testify about the effects on consumers of today's airline consolidation.

My name is Charles Leocha and I am the director of the Consumer Travel Alliance, a non-profit created to keep the needs of consumers in front of legislators, regulators and their staff. Our alliance is a member of the Consumer Federation of America. We are intimately involved with the current conference committee negotiation over the FAA Reauthorization. We are also working with state regulators, the FTC and DOT on privacy issues, travel insurance, pressing consumer issues with online and traditional travel agents and in the area of travel rights.

My testimony today focuses on the effects of the merger of United Airlines and Continental Airlines. I will also address the ongoing effects of consolidation in the airline industry that has been taking place for more than a decade. I am not speaking only for leisure travelers who make up more than 80 percent of airline passengers, but also for business travelers who provide more than 50 percent[1] of airline revenues.

Though these two airlines have many cooperative agreements, they still compete aggressively with each other in many ways — for corporate and leisure travelers, airline gates, frequent fliers, suppliers, travel agency attention and more.

We believe the Department of Justice and Congress should conclude that the proposed merger is not in the public interest, just as they did in June of last year, when reviewing the application from these same two carriers for airline alliance antitrust immunity.[2]

DOJ's reasons for denial included consumer harm, higher fares and elimination of competition, and ultimately that it was not in the public interest. Those same concerns resonate with this corporate marriage, but this union ups the ante — approval would make a third domestic merger almost inevitable.

THE ROAD TO THREE BIG CARRIERS

Should this merger be approved, the nation's system of network carriers will be effectively reduced to three major players — Delta, United and, perhaps, a coming mega-carrier formed by the merger of American Airlines with another airline. Even without the American merger with another carrier, this Delta/United/American triumvirate would control more than 50 percent of the U.S. domestic available seat miles (ASMs) and revenue passenger miles (RPMs).[3] Their airline alliances would control 85 percent of international traffic.[4] That kind of consolidation might bode poorly for business travelers as well as leisure travelers and may lead to another industry with its major players considered "too big to fail."

A merged United-Continental initially would have about 90,000 employees and about 700 aircraft, which certainly means higher odds of government bailouts or assistance than if the carriers operated individually. On the other hand, today, if one of these two airlines crumbled, the national air transportation system would shudder, but hardly be crippled.

ARE THERE BENEFITS FOR CONSUMERS?

The Consumer Travel Alliance cannot find any tangible consumer benefits of this merger and the ongoing consolidation in the airline industry. There are no new destinations, no new savings passed on to passengers and ultimately consumers are faced with less competition and higher prices. Consolidation to this point has already made airline signaling of airfare changes easier. This merger will make the process of raising airfares even simpler. The continued application of fees and the unbundling of airfares will also accelerate with fewer airlines in competition with each other. The institution of fees for checked baggage, seat reservations, meals and more has been followed by airline after airline like a herd of wildebeests crossing a crocodile-infested river.

To be sure, there are plenty of corporate benefits — reducing the combined workforce, certain economies of scale and increasing bargaining power (at the expense of suppliers). But business and leisure travelers don't get anything more than what they have been experiencing through the already coordinated international schedules, shared frequent flier miles and awards and visitation privileges at airport clubs.

Even United and Continental spin-doctors are having trouble finding specific consumer benefits from the merger now under consideration. On their merger website, they have touted supposed consumer benefits that are nothing new. We have all seen the following platitudes they cite for decades[5] —

- World's Most Comprehensive Network
  In reality, this is no benefit for consumers. At best, the Continental/United network remains identical to the current network operative through the Star Alliance. Potentially, there will be consolidation of overlapping routes. Though few routes overlap, the final honest assessment is a reduced network and fewer choices for both business and leisure travelers.
  Just as Delta swore that it would not abandon its hub at Cincinnati, current Continental statements about the sanctity of their Cleveland operations must be taken

with a grain of salt. Everyone in this room realizes that the reduction of flights were made in Cincinnati and that future reductions of flights from Cleveland will be made because of consumer demand, or the lack thereof. However, without the merger of Delta with Northwest and the proposed merger of Continental with United, Cincinnati probably would still be thriving and there would be no discussions about downsizing Continental's Cleveland operations.

- World's Leading Airline
  When has this been a benefit to consumers? The combination will have the same planes it currently is flying. The merged carrier will have the same frequent flier program that is already aligned through alliance membership.

- Competitive Fares
  United/Continental claim that 92 percent of their top 50 major city routes have low-cost-carrier competition. That competition will guarantee low airfares. The real change in competition will be in the field of business travel. There, this consolidation will have drastic effects on corporation travel programs that depend on hubs where CO/UA price competition will be eliminated.
  When corporate travel departments are faced with both a new paradigm presented by this merger plus the developing might of international alliances that are beginning to negotiate as a single entity rather than as a dozen or more separate airlines, competition will be further degraded.

- Award-winning customer service
  If past history provides any gauge consumers can expect a decrease in overall customer service when highly rated Continental merges with poorly performing United Airlines. It appears certain the Continental passengers will see degradation in the service levels that they have come to expect.
  According to DOT's Airline Quality ratings that measure complaints, misdirected baggage and on-time arrivals, Continental has ranked at the top of the major airlines for the past three years (if we take out Northwest that merged with Delta). United Airlines has been mired near the bottom of the rankings for the past two years, only excelled in poor customer service by Delta that has not budged from last place even as it absorbed the former customer-service champion, Northwest Airlines.
  In fact, customer service will be an unknown as Continental's vaunted service is merged with United's marginal service; a chance of reduced morale among Continental employees as their contracts are reduced to meet United pay levels is expected. From the consumer point of view, this bigger-is-better argument has no basis in reality.
  Historically, airline mergers have created a quantum increase in customer service problems. Of course all of these problems can be "worked out," however they subject consumers to additional headaches and travel disruption. One of the most frustrating is the consolidation of passenger data. Every recent merger from the days of the Continental/People Express to the Delta/Northwest mergers has been fraught with IT problems.

- Industry-leading frequent flier program
  These programs are already merged from an award-city point of view. The most likely result of this merger will be a shift to more passenger-unfriendly rules such as

hefty co-pays for upgrades. Having these frequent flier programs consolidated will allow the Big 3 airlines to more easily make anti-consumer changes. Competition between frequent flier programs is another form of competition that will be eliminated.

The bottom line: If what has happened in the past provides a roadmap to consequences of this pending merger, Consumers will see no benefits and may face degraded service, less competition, more fees and higher prices. Plus, possible changes to current frequent flier rules may raise mileage costs for redemption of miles and reduce free travel opportunities rather than increase them.

AIRLINE CONSOLIDATION BY MERGER

This proposed merger of United Airlines and Continental Airlines is the latest portion in a continuum of airline consolidation that has been slowly taking place over the past decade.

Mergers have been with the airline business for decades, however the size of these mergers is now creating airline behemoths that couldn't even be contemplated only a decade ago. Continental merged with People Express, Northwest merged with Republic, US Air merged with Allegheny, American merged with Reno Air and then TWA and last year Delta merged with Northwest to create what is the world's largest airline.

Now, Continental and United stand before the Department of Justice and Congress with a merger that will create even a larger airline.

AIRLINE ALLIANCE CONSOLIDATION

As domestic airlines have been merging, internationally mergers have also taken place. However, the granting of antitrust immunity that allows certain airlines to do unrestricted business together has changed the economic playing field.

It started with the granting of antitrust immunity for Northwest Airlines and KLM Airlines back in the early 199 0s in order to encourage European countries to negotiate Open Skies agreements with the U.S. This initial antitrust immunity grant was issued in the "public interest" for a greater good.

However, airlines discovered that antitrust immunity added significantly to the bottom line and though, today, we have Open Skies agreements with most European countries, the alliance antitrust immunity has continued to grow, not for the public good, but for corporate good.

These antitrust immunity grants have accelerated with the creation of three major airline alliances between the world's largest carriers. Lufthansa, United, US Airways, and Singapore airlines and others form the Star Alliance. American Airlines, British Airways, Iberia, Finnair, Qantas and others make up the OneWorld alliance. Delta, Northwest, Air France, KLM, Korean Air and others have created SkyTeam. Already, DOT has granted SkyTeam and Star Alliance antitrust immunity and the OneWorld alliance has applied for similar antitrust immunity.

This antitrust immunity allows alliance airlines to work together as a joint venture with a separate board of directors. Alliances are already jointly coordinating flights, schedules, route planning, marketing efforts, advertising, sales campaigns, frequent flier programs, catering and maintenance. These alliances are defacto mergers of the alliance's international business.

AN INCREASE IN AIRFARES

This merger needs to be looked at far more expansively than simply overlaying one route structure over another and then congratulating each other at the lack of overlapping routes. I admit that there are few overlapping routes between these airlines. When competition is taken out of the market it affects every route that an airline flies whether it overlaps with its merger partner or not. Investigators also need to examine non-stop flight markets as a separate and distinct market from connecting flights between city pairs.

Consider These Scenarios

First: With one less major network carrier, in an oligopolistic industry, the airline system of trial airfares has one less player. With one less "veto vote" available to reject system-wide fare increases the chances of consumers having to pay more in terms of airfares and airline fees increases exponentially.

Second: The merger also needs to be examined in light of today's airline alliances that already give Continental/United a joint venture for their transatlantic, Latin American and transpacific schedules and route structures. These joint ventures provide this merged carrier a government-approved system to profit from limited international competition and then use that profit to squeeze domestic competitors who do not have such government-assisted antitrust immunity provisions that virtually guarantee profits on international routes.

EFFECTIVE BUSINESS TRAVEL MONOPOLIES AT SELECT HUBS

The effects of the United/Continental merger will have far-reaching negative consequences for business as well as leisure travelers if it leads to a consolidation of the network airlines into three groups. When one of these mega-carriers controls the hub of a corporation, there is no competitive mega-carrier to limit the dominant hub airline's pricing power. Corporate air travel buyers will be forced to capitulate. This situation gets even worse when the dominant hub airline is linked with an international alliance and that alliance demands that corporations bargain with the alliance as a single joint venture rather than playing one airline off against another.

This kind of dominant hub power allows the mega-carrier to control prices for consumers and commissions that they pay travel agents. It affects far more than only business and leisure travelers. It affects new competition as well. Entry into a route that is anchored by a major carrier hub on both ends is extremely difficult for would-be competitors. Suppliers also face the difficulty of bargaining with the dominant mega-carrier from a real position of weakness. The resulting situation is anti-small-business in the hub airport community.

These major carriers also use mergers as a way to consolidate control of airport gates and in some cases take-off and landing slots. These kinds of gate and slot controls can make penetration by low cost carriers very difficult. Washington Reagan only recently has seen new low cost carriers (JetBlue will start up in November) because of limited take-off and landing slots.

At Boston Logan Airport, AirTran's operations were limited for months because they could only secure one gate while Northwest hoarded its gates simply to keep competition out of the airport. As we hold this hearing, Southwest Airlines is attempting to gain slots at both La Guardia and Washington Reagan so that they can compete with entrenched network carriers.

While many analysts and airline CEOs claim that three is the perfect number of large network competing airlines, that perfection in terms of competition only works if all three airlines have relatively equal strength across all markets. When market power is allowed to be concentrated in different hubs, the system is really a divide-and-conquer strategy. This fortress hub system is being played in every city where mega-carriers face minimal competition — Houston, Detroit, Minneapolis, and Dallas. Cities where two competing network carriers have hubs see much healthier competition — New York City, Los Angeles, Chicago.

LOWCOST CARRIERS, THE COMPETITION ANTIDOTE

The only real airline pricing discipline is generated by competition from low-cost carriers. The travel industry has documented the "Southwest Effect." This is a three- step effect where firstly, lower fares increase demand; secondly, competing airlines match the Southwest fares; and thirdly, sales rise for all airlines in the market.

This kind of competition can only take place if there are available gates at airports and available take-off and landing slots. Both factors must be considered carefully by DOJ while examining this pending merger as well, just as DOT has when considering recently proposed take-off/landing slot swaps between airlines.

On the transatlantic front, Open Skies agreements with the European Union (E.U.) may offer potential avenues for effective low-cost airline penetration when the low- cost airlines decide to expand internationally. Just as low-cost airlines began their move into the domestic market by serving less-popular airports, their expansion into transatlantic flying is dependent on a good Open Skies agreement since major hubs — Heathrow, Frankfurt, Amsterdam, Paris and Madrid — are locked up by the mega-airline alliances.

CONCLUSIONS

From a consumer perspective, this continued consolidation may be helping large airlines survive in the short run but when the economy improves, consumers — both leisure and business — will be left at the mercy of a government-approved system of airline oligopoly with less competition and, as a result, according to Department of Justice analysis, ultimately higher airfares.

In the short term, approval of this merger may not be seen as anti-competitive, but as a form of welfare for struggling airline corporations. In the long term, there is no doubt that effective airline competition will be eliminated and that a market with less competition is less consumer friendly.

If airline consolidation is allowed to continue along its current path with mergers of domestic carriers and antitrust arrangements for groups of international airlines, the Consumer Travel Alliance predicts this committee will find itself, within the decade, meeting to find ways to restore competition to airline system that is being eliminated today.

End Notes

[1] PhocusWright
[2] Jointapplication to Amend Order 2007-2-16 under 49 U.S.C. §§41308 and 41309 so as to Approve and Confer Antitrust Immunity, Comments of the Department of Justice on the Show Cause Order Docket OST-2008-0234 pg. 42
[3] AirlineForcasts.com Commentary: United + Continental is a big win for all stakeholders by Paul Mifsud, Carlos Bonilla, Vaughn Cordle, CFA
[4] Bureau of Transportation Statistics
[5] http://www.unitedcontinentalmerger.com/benefits/customers

In: Airline Industry Mergers: Background and Issues
Editor: Felix J. Mercado

ISBN: 978-1-61761-993-9
© 2011 Nova Science Publishers, Inc.

Chapter 7

TESTIMONY OF DANIEL MCKENZIE OF HUDSON SECURITIES, BEFORE THE COMMITTEE ON COMMERCE, SCIENCE & TRANSPORTATION, HEARING ON "THE FINANCIAL STATE OF THE AIRLINE INDUSTRY AND THE IMPLICATIONS OF CONSOLIDATION"

"Mr Chairman and members of the Senate here today, so thank you. As background, I have been helping investors analyze the airline industry for 10 years and my firm does not seek investment banking business from the airlines.

As has been widely reported and recognized, the US airline industry, with the exception of low cost carriers, has been a financial failure. We've successive decades. And if there is one that fact that the industry is structured one, and there are a number of reasons for why this ahead.

The second key point I want to leave with to my first point. As long as there are low cost carriers with a 20-30% cost advantage, they are going to try and undercut legacy carrier pricing and take market share. And I don't see this changing over my day we no longerhorizon. have a competitive industry is the day every airline has the same cost structure. However, low cost carriers, which today enjoy widespread brand acceptance, have been able to sustain sizeable cost advantages and through discounting, drive a shakeout among the legacy carriers, a phenomenon that will continue for the next several years.

The third point I want to leave you with is that the industry is on the financial mend, but it remains vulnerable to another spike in crude or another economic downturn. My outlook assumes average ticket prices rise 12% this year and 5% next year, which positions the industry to finally begin reporting modest profits. My forecast will naturally fluctuate based on the macro backdrop.

So what are factors that have caused the industry to suffer so much? Industry fragmentation is one key reason. If looking at capacity, the top 4 airlines in 2000 controlled 66% of industry capacity. That rose to 70% in 2005 and remains the case today. After the announced United and Continental merger, the top 4 airlines would control 81%.

But perhaps the easiest way to think about the terms of the real estate crisis. People case of the airline industry, airlines easily, go out and buy new planes, which over the past 32 years, has led to brutal competition.

Separately, the macro backdrop has hit the industry hard. The reality is, fleet and personnel plans made years ago could not have possibly anticipated the demand shock following the calamity of 9/11; a super spike in crude to $147; the recent financial meltdown; or worldwide health pandemics. Just as the tech bubble, the telecom bubble, the real estate bubble, and even the commodities bubble have burst, there has been a capacity bubble in the US Airline industry which today, is beginning to deflate as a consequence macro backdrop volatility. The industry has been undergoing a painful transformation over the past 32 years andn the 7th inning.

Some may wonder if deregulation 32 years too many benefits to cite. Recall that deregulation in the US has led to deregulation globally. Boeing, Airbus, all of their suppliers naturally; the banks; aircraft leasing companies; the gaming & lodging industry; and Travel Management Companies have all been very big winners.

So what does the future look like? The industry is not growing today, but there are orders for planes for delivery in 2012 and 2013, and the additional capacity will impact average ticket prices further out. Meanwhile, low cost carriers will continue to undercut on pricing and take market share. And separately, as long as management teams make promises to labor eep, we'll continue to see Ch. they can't k another Ch. 11 filing sometime in the next 5 years.

But there is one wild card here, and that's No. 1 threat to the finanical health of the industry. The debate on speculative trading in commodities is not whether it exists, but how best to remedy it. Unfortunately, the airline industry is a highly levered, high-fixed cost business that is reeling from 30% of its costs getting whipsawed by 50% in any given year. And the threat of another super spike has curtailed plane orders by many legacy carriers. Said differently, speculative trading is perverting capital spending and investment plans and as a result, is ultimately perverting economic growth.

I'll conclude by saying that there are a financial health of the industry. Demand is coming back and finances are improving, but there remain a number of structural challenges in place that will continue to make the recovery a slow process.

Mr Chairman and members of the Commerce Committee, thanks again for the opportunity to be here."

In: Airline Industry Mergers: Background and Issues
Editor: Felix J. Mercado

ISBN: 978-1-61761-993-9
© 2011 Nova Science Publishers, Inc.

Chapter 8

COMMERCIAL AVIATION: AIRLINE INDUSTRY CONTRACTION DUE TO VOLATILE FUEL PRICES AND FALLING DEMAND AFFECTING AIRPORTS, PASSENGERS, AND FEDERAL GOVERNMENT REVENUES

United States Government Accountability Office

WHY GAO DID THIS STUDY

The U.S. passenger airline industry is vital to the U.S. economy. Airlines directly generate billions of dollars in revenues each year and catalyze economic growth. Interest in the airlines' ability to weather volatile fuel prices and the economic recession led to congressional requests for a GAO review. GAO examined how (1) the financial condition of the U.S. passenger airline industry has changed, the principal factors affecting its condition, and its prospects for 2009; (2) airlines have responded to the factors affecting their financial condition; and (3) changes in the industry have affected airports, passengers, and the Airport and Airway Trust Fund (Trust Fund), which funds the Federal Aviation Administration's (FAA) capital programs and most of its operations. To do this, GAO analyzed financial and operating data, reviewed studies, and interviewed airline, airport, and FAA officials and other experts. The Department of Transportation (DOT) provided technical comments, which were incorporated as appropriate.

WHAT GAO RECOMMENDS

In light of the declining uncommitted balance in the Trust Fund, Congress should consider working with FAA to reduce the risk of overcommitting budgetary resources from the Trust Fund so that resources are available to cover all the obligations that FAA has the authority to incur and reduce the risk of disruptions in funds for aviation programs and projects.

WHAT GAO FOUND

After 2 years of profits, the U.S. passenger airline industry lost $4.3 billion in the first 3 quarters of 2008—the most currently available financial data— largely due to volatile fuel prices. Losses grew as jet fuel prices increased 60 percent over 2007 levels by midyear, only to tumble rapidly to about one-third of the year's high by year-end. While early 2009 forecasts suggested a return to profitability, largely due to lower fuel prices, the deepening recession has cast doubt on those predictions. The demand for air travel now appears to be weaker than expected—especially among business and international travelers—and revenues appear to be declining. Today, the outlook for the industry's profitability in 2009 is uncertain.

U.S. airlines responded to volatile fuel prices and then a weakening economy by cutting their capacity, reducing their fleets and workforces, and instituting new fees. Collectively, U.S. airlines reduced domestic capacity, as measured by the number of seats flown, by about 9 percent from the fourth quarter of 2007 to the fourth quarter of 2008. Most of these cuts remain in place. To reduce capacity, airlines reduced the overall number of active aircraft in their fleets by 18 percent by eliminating mostly older, less fuel-efficient, and smaller (50 or fewer seats) aircraft. Airlines also collectively reduced their workforces by about 28,000, or nearly 7 percent, from the end of 2007 to the end of 2008, but further downsizing is expected in 2009. In addition to reducing capacity, most airlines instituted new fees, such as those for checked baggage, which resulted in $635 million during the first 3 quarters of 2008.

The contraction of the U.S. airline industry in 2008 reduced airport revenues, passengers' access to the national aviation system, and revenues for the Trust Fund. Domestic passenger traffic, as measured by enplanements, decreased by 9 percent overall, but by more than 25 percent at some airports, from the fourth quarter of 2007 to the fourth quarter of 2008. With this decrease, airport revenues declined, prompting airports to reduce their operating costs and delay capital improvement projects. Despite the drop in traffic and revenues, airports are generally considered financially sound owing to considerable cash reserves. However, airline capacity reductions are causing some passengers to lose some or all access to commercial air service and contributing to increased fares in some passenger markets. Small airports, which already offer fewer flight options, had the greatest percentage decrease in nonstop destinations (16 percent) as well as a 10 percent reduction in capacity. Additionally, 38 airports lost all service from the fourth quarter of 2007 to the fourth quarter of 2008—roughly twice the number that lost all service for the same periods in 2006 and 2007. With the industry's contraction, Trust Fund revenues fell, contributing to a decline in the fund's uncommitted balance. Appropriations from the Trust Fund are based on FAA's projected revenues, and actual revenues have been less than FAA's forecast, resulting in the uncommitted balance falling from about $7.3 billion at the end of fiscal year 2001 to about $1.4 billion at the end of fiscal year 2008, and may fall further. If the uncommitted balance declines close to zero, FAA might have to delay capital programs unless additional funding is made available.

ABBREVIATIONS

AIP	Airport Improvement Program
DOT	Department of Transportation
EAS	Essential Air Service
FAA	Federal Aviation Administration
OAG	Official Airline Guide
PFC	passenger facility charges
SEC	Securities and Exchange Commission

April 21, 2009

The Honorable John D. Rockefeller, IV
Chairman
The Honorable Kay Bailey Hutchison
Ranking Member
Committee on Commerce, Science, and Transportation
United States Senate

The Honorable John L. Mica
Ranking Republican Member
Committee on Transportation and Infrastructure
House of Representatives

The Honorable Thomas E. Petri
Ranking Member
Subcommittee on Aviation
Committee on Transportation and Infrastructure
House of Representatives

The U.S. passenger airline industry is vital to the U.S. economy. Airlines directly generate billions of dollars in revenues each year, catalyze economic growth, and influence the quality of peoples' lives around the globe. Communities, both large and small, depend on airlines to help connect them to the national transportation system which links economies and promotes the exchange of people, products, and ideas. The downturn in the airline industry that followed the terrorist attacks of September 11, 2001, adversely affected passengers, employees, suppliers, and communities. While U.S. airlines eventually rebounded from that downturn, 2008 presented fresh challenges to the industry in the form of record-high fuel prices and an economic recession. During the first half of 2008, seven smaller U.S. passenger airlines liquidated.

Because of your interest in the capability of U.S. passenger airlines to weather these financial challenges, you asked us to provide an update on the financial condition of the airline industry. To address these issues, we examined how (1) the financial condition of the U.S. passenger airline industry has changed, the principal factors affecting its condition, and its prospects for 2009; (2) airlines have responded to the factors affecting their financial condition; and (3) changes in the passenger airline industry have affected airports, passengers, and the federal Airport and Airway Trust Fund (Trust Fund), which funds the Federal Aviation Administration (FAA).

To address these objectives, we analyzed Department of Transportation (DOT) financial and operating data, reviewed historical documents and past studies, and conducted interviews. Specifically, to evaluate how the financial condition of the U.S. passenger airline industry has changed, the principal factors affecting its condition, and its prospects for 2009, we analyzed airline financial indicators, reviewed financial studies, and interviewed airline managers, trade association officials, financial analysts, and other industry experts. Our financial analysis relied on airline financial data reported to DOT by airlines from 2005 through the first 3 quarters of 2008—the most recently available data from DOT.[1] All dollar figures in this chapter are nominal unless otherwise noted. To determine how airlines have responded to the factors affecting their financial condition, we analyzed airline schedule data from BACK Aviation Solution's Official Airline Guide (OAG),[2] spoke with airline officials and industry experts, and reviewed airline financial statements. To assess how changes in the U.S. passenger airline industry have affected airports, passengers, and the Trust Fund, we conducted 12 case studies of large, medium, small, and nonhub airports from different regions;[3] analyzed DOT enplanement and fare data and OAG schedule data; spoke with airport consultants, FAA officials, and industry associations; and reviewed DOT data on the Trust Fund. To assess the reliability of the DOT and OAG data, we reviewed the quality control procedures applied by DOT and BACK Aviation and determined that the data were sufficiently reliable for our purposes. We conducted this performance audit from July 2008 through April 2009 in accordance with generally accepted government auditing standards. Those standards require that we plan and perform the audit to obtain sufficient, appropriate evidence to provide a reasonable basis for our findings and conclusions based on our audit objectives. We believe that the evidence obtained provides a reasonable basis for our findings and conclusions based on our audit objectives. See appendix I for more information on our scope and methodology.

We provided a draft of this chapter to DOT for review and comment. DOT officials provided some clarifying and technical comments, which we incorporated where appropriate.

BACKGROUND

The U.S. airline industry is principally composed of legacy, low-cost, and other airlines, and although it is largely free of economic regulation, it remains regulated in other areas, most notably safety, security, and operating standards. Legacy airlines—sometimes called network airlines—are essentially those airlines that were in operation before the Airline Deregulation Act of 1978 and whose goal is to provide service from "anywhere to everywhere." To meet that goal, these airlines support large, complex hub-and-spoke operations with thousands of employees and hundreds of aircraft (of various types), with service at numerous fare levels to domestic communities of all sizes and to international destinations. To enhance revenues without expending capital, legacy airlines have entered into domestic (and international) alliances that give them access to some portion of each others' networks. Low-cost airlines generally entered the marketplace after deregulation and tend to operate less costly point-to-point service using fewer types of aircraft. Low-cost airlines typically offer simplified fare structures, which were originally aimed at leisure passengers but are increasingly attractive to business passengers because they typically have less restrictive ticketing rules. These restrictions often make it significantly more expensive to purchase tickets within 2 weeks of the flight or make changes to an existing itinerary. Other airlines include regional and niche airlines that tend not to offer national service but instead specialize in certain markets and destinations. Regional airlines operate smaller aircraft—turboprops or regional jets with up to 100 seats—and generally provide service under code-sharing arrangements with larger legacy airlines on a cost-plus or fee-for-departure basis to smaller communities. Some regional airlines are owned by a legacy parent, while others are independent.[4] For example, American Eagle is the regional subsidiary for American Airlines, while independent Sky West Airlines operates on a fee-per-departure agreement with Delta Air Lines, United Airlines, and Midwest Airlines.

Since the airline industry was deregulated in 1978, its earnings have been extremely volatile. In fact, despite considerable periods of strong growth and increased earnings, airlines have at times suffered such substantial financial distress that many have filed for bankruptcy and the industry as a whole has failed to earn sufficient returns to cover capital costs in the long run. Some academics and industry analysts view the industry as inherently unstable because of key demand and cost characteristics. Most notably, the demand for air travel is highly cyclical in relation to the state of the economy as well as to political, international, and even health-related events, but the cost characteristics of the industry can make it difficult for carriers to very quickly match the supply of air service to quickly shifting demand.

Table 1. Sources of Airport Funding, 2001 through 2005

2006 dollars in billions			
Funding source	2001-2005 average annual funding	Percentage of total	Source of funds
Airport bonds	$6.5[a]	50	State and local governments or airport authorities issue tax-exempt debt
AIP grants	3.6[b]	29	Congress makes funds available from the Trust Fund, which receives revenue from various aviation-related taxes
Passenger facility charges	2.2[c]	17	Funds come from passenger fees of up to $4.50 per trip segment at commercial airports[d]
State and local contributions	0.7	4	Funds include state and local grants, loans, and matching funds for AIP grants
Total	**$13**	**100**	

Source: GAO analysis of FAA, Thomson Financial, and state grant data.
[a]Net of refinancing.
[b]AIP totaled on a fiscal year basis.
[c]As much as $660 million (30 percent of total) of which is used to support bond financing.
[d]49 U.S.C. § 40117.

Passengers access airlines in the United States through any of 517 commercial service airports.[5] FAA further divides commercial service airports into primary airports (enplaning more than 10,000 passengers annually) and other commercial service airports. The 382 primary airports are arranged into various classes of hub airports—large, medium, small, and nonhub—based on passenger traffic.[6] Passenger traffic is highly concentrated: 69 percent of passengers enplaned at the 30 large hub airports and another 20 percent enplaned at the 37 medium hub airports in 2007. Airports finance their operations and capital development from a variety of sources. Operations are financed through airline and other aviation-related fees and from passenger and other revenues. Capital development for runways, terminals, and other projects is financed through an even wider variety of sources, including municipal bonding, federal Airport Improvement Program (AIP) grants, passenger facility charges (PFC), and state and local government contributions. As we last estimated in 2007, total airport capital financing averaged $13 billion annually from 2001 through 2005.[7] (See table 1.)

Large and medium hub airports, which together handle almost 90 percent of passenger traffic, accounted for 72 percent of all airport capital funding. Airport financing varies according to the size of the airport. Large and medium hub airports rely principally on airport bonds and PFCs for funding, while smaller airports rely principally on AIP grants, which are funded through the Trust Fund, for their capital development.[8]

The Trust Fund is the exclusive source of funding for FAA's capital programs, including AIP, and is also used to fund FAA's operations account. In addition, General Fund contributions from the Treasury supplement Trust Fund revenues for operations and have constituted roughly 8 to 24 percent of FAA's total appropriation since fiscal year 2000. Trust Fund revenues stem principally from excise taxes on the purchase of airline tickets and fuel and the shipment of air cargo and are available to FAA for use subject to appropriation.[9] Starting with AIR-21 in 2000[10] and continuing with Vision 100[11] in 2003, Congress has based FAA's fiscal year appropriation from the Trust Fund on the forecasted level of Trust Fund revenues, including interest on Trust Fund balances, as set forth in the President's baseline budget projection for the coming fiscal year. FAA generates a forecast for the President's budget using models based on historical relationships between key economic variables, such as the growth rate of the economy, and aviation measures, such as passenger traffic levels and passenger fares, that affect Trust Fund revenues. This forecast, and accordingly FAA's appropriation, is based on information available in the first quarter of the preceding fiscal year.

U.S. PASSENGER AIRLINE INDUSTRY'S FINANCIAL CONDITION WEAKENED IN 2008 BECAUSE OF VOLATILE FUEL PRICES AND FALLING DEMAND AND ITS PROSPECTS FOR 2009 ARE UNCERTAIN

After 2 Years of Profits, Airline Industry Lost $4.3 Billion through the First 3 Quarters of 2008

The airline industry incurred operating losses of $4.3 billion in the first 3 quarters of 2008 after earning operating profits of about $5.2 billion in 2006 and $6.9 billion in 2007. The airlines' fourth quarter 2008 financial results are expected to deepen the total losses for the year. For example, 11 airlines that comprise about 75 percent of the industry's total operating revenues in 2008 reported losses of $2.4 billion in the fourth quarter of 2008 to the SEC.[12] The airline industry's financial performance over the past 2 decades demonstrates the industry's historically cyclical nature. (See Figure 1.)

The airline industry's cyclical profits are caused by the airlines' inability to quickly adjust the supply of air service. For example, while demand for air travel is particularly sensitive to changes in the economy and world events like the terrorist attacks of September 11, 2001,[13] the cost characteristics of the industry make it difficult for firms to rapidly adjust to changes in demand. In particular, aircraft are expensive, long-lived capital assets, therefore, if demand changes quickly, airlines may find it difficult to quickly change the size of their aircraft fleets. Additionally, passengers book flights months in advance, further complicating near-term efforts to reduce capacity. Moreover, even though labor is generally viewed as a variable cost, airline employees are mostly unionized, and airlines find that they may not be able to quickly and significantly reduce employment costs when demand for air travel changes. These cost characteristics can thus lead to considerable excess capacity during periods of declining demand—which would likely result in declining profits. Conversely, if demand rises, it can be difficult for airlines to expand very rapidly, which could lead to increases in airfares and profits. At times though, airlines make relatively quick shifts in their capacity in response to changed circumstances. For example, the substantial drop-off in demand after September 11 led to a relatively swift 14 percent reduction in legacy airline capacity in the fourth quarter of 2001 as compared to the same quarter 1 year earlier. Nevertheless, the underlying fundamental characteristics of the industry suggest that it will likely remain susceptible to rapid swings in its financial health.

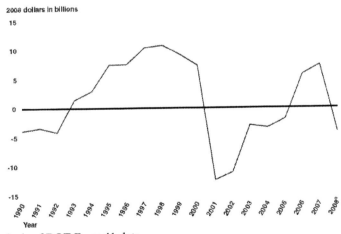

Source: GAO analysis of DOT Form 41 data.

Note: Since the 11 largest airlines reported losses of $2.4 billion in the fourth quarter of 2008 to the SEC, the losses for 2008 are likely understated in this graphic because fourth quarter of 2008 is not included. Also, since this graphic covers a long time period, we adjusted these numbers for inflation.

[a]The data for 2008 represent only the first 3 quarters of the year.

Figure 1. Annual Operating Profit and Loss for U.S. Passenger Airlines, 1990 through the First 3 Quarters of 2008

Volatile Jet Fuel Prices Contributed to Losses in 2008

Increases in the price of jet fuel—the airlines' biggest operating expense in 2008—were the chief contributor to airline losses in 2008. In the first 3 quarters of 2007, jet fuel costs were 25 percent of total airline expenses, but grew to 32 percent of total expenses in the same period in 2008. By the third quarter of 2008, jet fuel prices increased 60 percent over 2007 levels. Seven smaller airlines ceased operations during the first half of the year and others entered bankruptcy, in large part because of high fuel prices.[14] Moreover, although the market price of jet fuel began to fall during the third quarter of 2008, actual prices paid for jet fuel did not fall as quickly because of airlines' prepaid fuel contracts, or fuel hedges. (See Figure 2.)

Airlines have used fuel hedges to reduce the effects of fuel price volatility on their earnings, but the airlines' fuel hedges resulted in losses when fuel prices rapidly fell at the end of 2008. With fuel hedging, airlines enter into varied types of contracts that are designed to provide more certainty over the future price of fuel and thus help to manage the airlines' future costs. The fuel hedging strategies that airlines have used were initially beneficial in 2008 because the contracts they had entered into gave them protection against increases in the price of fuel, which occurred in early 2008 through the summer.[15] However, when fuel prices tumbled rapidly to about one-third of the year's highest price at the end of 2008, many airlines incurred substantial losses because their hedging strategies involved substantial downside risk—that is, they were exposed to financial losses in the event of a sharp decline in the price of fuel.[16] Several airlines' cash balances were adversely affected because they had to set aside collateral to cover the losses they were incurring on their fuel hedges. As a result of lower fuel prices that currently exist and the losses they recently incurred on hedge contracts, airlines have reduced the extent to which they are hedged in 2009.[17]

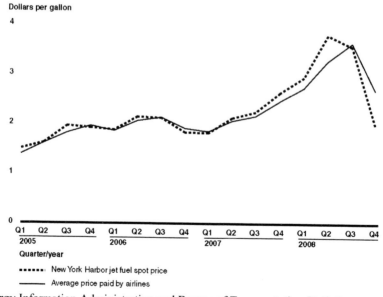

Sources: Energy Information Administration and Bureau of Transportation Statistics.

Figure 2. U.S. Jet Fuel Spot Prices and Passenger Airline Price Paid for U.S. Jet Fuel, First Quarter 2005 through Fourth Quarter 2008

Airline Revenues Improved in 2008 despite Declines in Passenger Traffic

During the 12-month period encompassing the fourth quarter of 2007 through the third quarter of 2008, total airline operating revenues increased by approximately $12.8 billion, or about 9 percent, over the similar 12-month period in the previous year.[18] (See Figure 3.)

The rise in airline revenues in 2008 was largely driven by increases in airfares (as measured by yields, or the amount of revenue airlines collect for every mile a passenger travels).[19] While passenger traffic (as measured by revenue passenger miles)[20] grew during the first quarter of 2008 compared to first quarter 2007 levels, passenger traffic began to decline year-over-year during the second quarter and by the fourth quarter was down almost 8 percent as compared to the fourth quarter of 2007. However, several factors mitigated the effect of this traffic decline on revenues. During the early part of the year, yields were rising rapidly largely due to higher fares by carriers to help cover their increased fuel expenses. Thus, even when traffic began to decline year-over-year in the second quarter, revenues were rising significantly over their level in the second quarter of 2007. By the third and fourth quarter of 2008, when traffic fell off more significantly, airlines began to reduce capacity, which enabled airlines to maintain relatively high load factors—that is, a high percentage of seats filled. On average, over 80 percent of available seats were filled in the third quarter of 2008—one of the highest levels in the past decade. One airline industry expert told us that as long as many flights are full or nearly full, airlines can maintain relatively high yields. As figure 4 shows, airlines continued to reduce domestic capacity year-over-year throughout 2008 (as measured by available seat-miles), and yields continued to rise through the third quarter of 2008—the most recently available data from DOT.

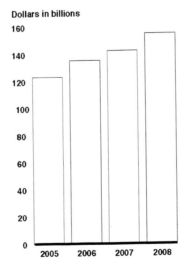

Source: GAO analysis of DOT Form 41 data.

Note: The data for 2005 represent the 12-month period encompassing the fourth quarter of 2004 through the third quarter of 2005; 2006 represents the fourth quarter of 2005 through the third quarter of 2006; 2007 represents the fourth quarter of 2006 through the third quarter of 2007; and 2008 represents the fourth quarter of 2007 through the third quarter of 2008.

Figure 3. U.S. Airline Industry's Total Operating Revenue, 12-Month Periods Starting with Fourth Quarter 2004 through Third Quarter 2008

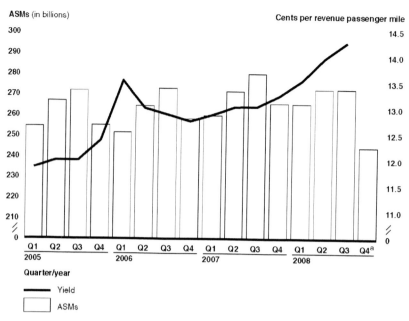

Source: GAO analysis of DOT Form 41 data.

[a]Yields for the fourth quarter 2008 are not yet available from DOT, but according to the Air Transport Association's sample of seven airlines, domestic passenger yields fell 0.2 percent and 1.3 percent in November and December 2008, respectively.

Figure 4. U.S. Airline Industry Capacity and Yields, First Quarter 2005 through Fourth Quarter 2008

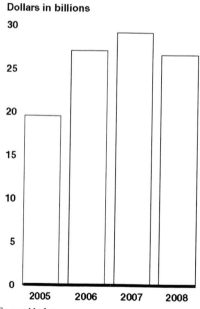

Source: GAO analysis of DOT Form 41 data.

Note: The data represent the total liquidity (cash and short-term investments) for the third quarter of each year.

Figure 5. Liquidity for the U.S. Airlines, Third Quarter 2005 through Third Quarter 2008

Early indications are that fourth quarter 2008 yields have leveled off or fallen, though DOT data are not yet available. More recently, fares and yields have begun to decline in 2009 as demand has continued to fall.

Airlines' Liquidity Deteriorated in 2008 due to Volatile Fuel Prices

Over the past 3 years, U.S. passenger airlines improved their collective liquidity from a total of $18.6 billion at the start of 2005 to $28.1 billion at the end of 2007, but with the high fuel prices their cash reserves deteriorated to about $26.6 billion by the third quarter of 2008. (See Figure 5.) Greater liquidity improves a firm's ability to meet short-term liabilities with cash or marketable securities. Liquidity levels are especially important in the airline industry because cash balances help the airlines withstand potential future industry shocks, such as changes in demand or fuel prices, as well as pay down debt and reduce the risk of bankruptcy.

U.S. airlines are expected to report a further deterioration in their liquidity levels in the fourth quarter of 2008 as a result of losses on fuel hedges. For example, the 11 largest airlines reported to the SEC approximately $18 billion in liquidity for the fourth quarter of 2008, down from approximately $24 billion in the third quarter of 2008.

In 2008, the 11 largest airlines raised an estimated $8 billion in capital from a variety of sources, including advance frequent flyer mileage sales to credit card companies, equity and debt issuance, and asset sales.[21] For example, Delta Air Lines and American Express executed a credit card deal that boosted Delta's cash position by $1 billion. Continental Airlines generated $149 million by selling its interest in Copa Holdings (Airlines), while Southwest Airlines secured aircraft mortgage financing from seven European banks for $600 million. Even in Chapter 11 reorganization, Frontier Airlines was able to line up $30 million in financing from a group of lenders, including Republic Airways. These airlines' actions to improve liquidity lessened the possibility of their breaking debt covenants or facing bankruptcy and helped the airlines weather the increase in fuel prices. In the coming months, airlines may seek to sell or exchange other assets to increase their liquidity. However, airline analysts noted most airlines exhausted their available options to generate cash in 2008 and have limited cash-generating opportunities in 2009. Additionally, some analysts noted that sources of aircraft capital, such as the sale and leaseback of aircraft, are largely inaccessible, because of current credit market conditions. However, analysts believe that if fuel prices remain at or near current levels, the airlines will have sufficient cash flow to avoid depleting their cash balances.

The Industry's Financial Health in 2009 Is Uncertain due to the Current Recession, Labor Costs, Debt, and Pension Obligations

The U.S. passenger airline industry's potential profitability in 2009 is uncertain due to the current recession.[22] At the beginning of 2009, some airlines and airline financial analysts forecast a return to profits for this year, primarily because of the dramatic decrease in fuel prices. For example, two analysts estimated profits of around $4 billion to $10 billion based on the assumption that jet fuel prices will remain low—around $55 to $62 per barrel of oil—

and revenues would fall around 4.5 percent to 7 percent; however, the fuel savings will offset any declines in revenues due to reduced traffic and fares. Other analysts forecast revenue declines of 4 to 8 percent in 2009 based on deteriorating passenger demand. One Wall Street analyst estimated that at current fuel prices, airline revenues would have to fall over 12 percent before the airlines would incur losses—a decline that would constitute a worse revenue environment than existed immediately after September 11, 2001. Additionally, another analyst estimated that an 8 to 12 percent decline in revenues would require economic growth, as measured by the gross domestic product, to fall at an unprecedented rate. However, even if the airline industry generates modest operating profits in 2009, it is unlikely to cover its cost of capital.

Despite earlier optimism regarding airline profitability for 2009, the situation now seems to be worsening. Early indications on bookings and revenues for the first 2 quarters of the year suggest that demand will be weaker than had been expected at the beginning of 2009. Analysts and some airlines are now seeing demand significantly weaken among their highest-paying customers—business and international travelers. Additionally, initial reports show that load factors are beginning to fall, and fares are declining. As such, prospects for a profitable year have become more uncertain.

Even if the airline industry generates an operating profit in 2009, its financial health is still under pressure from potentially higher costs for labor, one of the airlines' major expenses, in the coming years. According to labor union representatives, nearly every labor contract at every major airline is currently open or amendable by the end of 2009, totaling 83 open labor contracts at 34 legacy, low-cost, and other airlines.[23] (See app. II.) In large part, this situation exists because so many contracts were restructured during or under the threat of bankruptcy in 2003 and 2004. Of the 83 open contracts, 42 are currently in mediation with the National Mediation Board (NMB).[24] Depending on whether NMB moves to settle these contracts, airlines may be compelled to settle at an increased cost. For example, Southwest Airlines recently came to a tentative agreement with its pilots' union that includes increased wages and retirement benefits.

Although lower fuel prices will reduce the demand on cash balances, airlines have long-term obligations, including debt maturities and required pension contributions that could strain their cash balances in the coming years. Fitch Ratings estimates that the seven largest U.S. airlines face a total of $4.4 billion in debt and capital lease maturities in 2009 and will have approximately $6 billion more coming due in 2010. Airline analysts believe that if fuel prices remain at or near current levels, the airlines' cash flow should improve, making it possible for airlines to cover payments on their debt in 2009. Additionally, some airlines with defined benefit pension plans expect to have higher pension expenses in 2009 compared to 2008 because the value of their plans' assets fell due to declining stock market conditions.[25] Furthermore, because of current market conditions, two of the airlines—Delta and Hawaiian—expect the 2010 funding requirements to significantly exceed 2009 requirements; these contributions could adversely affect the airlines' financial condition. However, the extent of these airlines' overall funding requirements in 2009 and 2010 will depend on a number of factors, including the plans' asset levels and returns and corporate interest rates used to measure liabilities, as well as changes in pension laws.[26]

AIRLINES ARE RESPONDING TO VOLATILE FUEL COSTS AND A WEAKENING ECONOMY BY REDUCING THEIR DOMESTIC CAPACITY

Airline Industry Reduced Domestic Capacity

In responding to high fuel prices and a weakening economy, the U.S. passenger airline industry reduced domestic capacity (the number of scheduled seats) in 2008 by the largest percentage since the 2001 terrorist attacks. The capacity cuts were designed to reduce costs and help to push up fares—or at least maintain fares—by limiting the supply of airline seats relative to the demand. Compared with the same quarter in 2007, the industry reduced domestic capacity by 9 percent in the fourth quarter 2008.[27] In comparison, during the 1991 and 2001-2002 industry contractions, airlines reduced their capacity by about 4 percent and 12 percent, respectively. In the fourth quarter of 2008, legacy airlines reduced domestic capacity by 10 percent, whereas low-cost airlines reduced their capacity by 4 percent, and other airlines reduced capacity by 35 percent as compared with the fourth quarter of 2007.[28] (See table 2.) These cuts have continued into 2009. Legacy airlines moved some of their domestic capacity to their international operations for which capacity fell by only 3 percent during 2008. As passenger traffic levels have fallen, some airlines have begun announcing further capacity cuts in 2009.

To Reduce Capacity, Airlines Adjusted the Composition and Size of Their Fleets

As U.S. airlines reduced their domestic capacity, they reduced the size of their active fleets by nearly 800 aircraft, or 18 percent, from 2007 to 2008 as well as changed the composition of their fleet.[29] The U.S. airline fleet is made up of four basic types of aircraft: widebody (twin aisle), narrowbody (single aisle), regional jets, and turboprops. According to schedule data submitted by the airlines, the airlines reduced their total available seats by about 22 million, or 9 percent, from the fourth quarter of 2007 to the fourth quarter of 2008 with the narrowbody aircraft accounting for 83 percent of this reduction.[30] However, the largest percentage reduction in seats (year over year) by a particular aircraft type occurred through the removal of widebody aircraft, such as 747s and A-330s, from domestic service. (See table 3.) Some legacy airlines shifted these aircraft to be used on international routes. Narrowbody aircraft, such as 737s and MD-80s, saw the second largest percentage reduction in capacity within a type of aircraft because these aircraft are older and less fuel efficient and therefore costlier to operate, especially when fuel costs are high, and we were told that many of these older aircraft are unlikely to return to service. For example, Alaska Airlines retired its entire fleet of MD-80s in 2008 and Continental Airlines retired many of its older generation 737 aircraft. Regional jets and turboprop planes, including the Embraer 175 regional jet and 76-seat DASH-8 Q400 turboprop, experienced the smallest percentage reduction in seat capacity by type of aircraft because airlines are switching to smaller aircraft on some routes in response to the decrease in passenger traffic.

**Table 2. Percentage Change in Scheduled Domestic Seats
(from Fourth Quarter 2007 to Fourth Quarter of 2008)**

Carrier type	Percentage change from 4th quarter 2007 to 4th quarter 2008	Percent of total seats (4th quarter 2008)
Legacy	-10	69
Low-cost carrier[a]	-4	28
Other[b]	**-35**	**3**

Source: GAO analysis of OAG data.

Note: Seats are based on one-way, nonstop flights. Also, totals may not equal 100 percent due to exclusion of airlines with less than 400,000 seats in the fourth quarter 2007.

[a]Liquidation of ATA accounted for 1 percentage point.

[b]Liquidation of Aloha Airlines accounted for 31 percentage points.

Error! Bookmark not defined.

**Table 3. Percentage Change in Seats, by Aircraft Type
(from Fourth Quarter of 2007 to Fourth Quarter of 2008)**

Body type	Percent of total capacity	Percentage change
Regional Jet	21	-4
Turboprop	4	-6
Narrowbody	72	-11
Widebody	3	-18
Total	100	-9

Source: GAO analysis of OAG data.

**Table 4. Percentage Change in Seats, by Seat Configuration
(from Fourth Quarter 2007 to Fourth Quarter 2008)**

Seat range	Percent of total capacity	Percentage change
<=50	15	-17
>=100	75	-11
51-99	10	23
Total	100	-9

Source: GAO analysis of OAG data.

In 2008, the airlines also changed the size of aircraft deployed in various markets. Most notably, while the regional jet and turboprop categories, which generally consist of aircraft with fewer than 100 seats, experienced a small percentage reduction in total seats by aircraft type, there was a marked shift from 50-seat and smaller aircraft to regional jets and turboprops with more than 50 seats. For example, the use of 70-seat Embraer 175 regional jet and 76-seat DASH-8 Q400 turboprop grew substantially, while many 50- and 37-seat regional jets and 19-seat turboprops were taken out of service in 2008. Smaller airports and communities that are linked as spokes to airline hubs such as Denver or Atlanta often rely on smaller aircraft (50 or fewer seats). Compared with the fourth quarter of 2007, capacity on smaller aircraft with 50 or fewer seats decreased by 17 percent in the fourth quarter of 2008.

Capacity on larger aircraft (51 to 99 seats) increased by 23 percent during the same period. In addition, across all hub types, capacity declined on aircraft with 50 or fewer seats while capacity increased on larger aircraft with 51 to 99 seats. (See table 4.)

Airlines Cancelled and Deferred Aircraft Orders and Deliveries as Capacity and Traffic Decline

In line with reducing capacity, some U.S. airlines cancelled or deferred future aircraft deliveries as they realigned their fleets in preparation for less capacity growth. For example, during 2008, low-cost airline AirTran Airways deferred its purchase of 18 aircraft originally scheduled for delivery from 2009 through 2010. Continental Airlines pushed back the delivery of two widebody aircraft from 2009 to 2010. JetBlue Airways delayed delivery of 21 narrowbody aircraft until 2014 and 2015.[31] While details of deferrals and cancellations are often not disclosed, other carriers may be seeking to delay or cancel orders in the current economic environment.

Workforce Reductions Have Followed Capacity Reductions and Reflect Financial Pressures on Airlines

In tandem with their capacity and fleet reductions, U.S. passenger airlines reduced their workforces. Since the middle of 2008, many airlines have announced job cuts as part of their capacity and cost reduction programs. U.S. airlines reduced their workforces by about 28,000 employees, or about 7 percent of total 391,918 employees from the fourth quarter of 2007 to the fourth quarter of 2008. The seven airlines that shut down in 2008 accounted for some of these reductions. For example, the shutdown of ATA resulted in a loss of over 2,300 employees. Employee reductions are common in the airline industry during industry contractions. During the 1991 and 2001 industry contractions, employment decreased between 5 percent and 12 percent, which was generally equal to the reduction in capacity.[32] Although the current employee reductions are less than the capacity cuts, the airlines, especially those that were previously in bankruptcy, may have already reduced employee levels, making further cuts difficult. However, the weakening economic climate will continue to push airlines to reduce more costs. In January 2009, United Airlines announced additional employee reductions by the end of 2009 in an attempt to reduce overhead costs.[33]

Airlines Raised Revenues through New Fees

Passenger airlines have increased fees for a variety of services, most notably for checked baggage. Specifically, five legacy and three low-cost airlines instituted a first-bag fee and all legacy airlines and all but one low-cost airline have imposed second-bag fees. (See table 5.) Almost all of these baggage fees were introduced during 2008. In addition, many airlines instituted other fees for services provided before or during a flight such as seat choice or a pillow kit.

Table 5. Legacy and Low-Cost Airlines' Checked Baggage Fees, as of February 2009

Airline	1st bag fee (one way)	2nd bag fee (one way)	3rd bag fee (one way)
Legacy			
Alaska	$0	$25	$125
American	15	25	100
Continental	15	25	100
Delta/Northwest	15	25	125
United	15	25	125
U.S. Airways	15	25	100
Low-cost airlines			
AirTran	15	25	50
JetBlue	0	20	75
Frontier	15	25	50
Southwest	0	0	25
Spirit	15-25	15-25	100

Source: Calyon Securities and company reports.

Note: Baggage fees are usually waived for frequent fliers with elite status. Other airlines have also implemented similar fees.

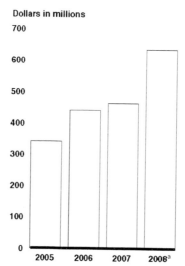

Source: GAO analysis of DOT Form 41 data.

[a]2005 through 2007 represent data for the four-quarter period. 2008 represents data for only the first 3 quarters of the year.

Figure 6. U.S. Airline Revenue Collected from Baggage Fees, 2005 through 2008

In 2008, the legacy and low-cost airlines generated about $8 billion in other revenues, which include fees for checked baggage, beverages, and food.[34] As figure 6 shows, revenue from excess baggage, including checked baggage fees, increased by 86 percent, from $341 million in 2005 to $635 million for the first 3 quarters of 2008.[35] While this revenue stream represented less than 1 percent of total operating revenues in 2008, it provided a new source of revenue for the airlines. Airlines and analysts expect these fees to remain and forecast that fee revenues are likely to increase substantially in 2009, despite reductions in passenger traffic, because many of the fees were not introduced until later in 2008.

AIRLINE INDUSTRY CONTRACTION AFFECTS AIRPORTS, PASSENGERS, AND FEDERAL GOVERNMENT REVENUES

Despite Declining Passenger Traffic, Airports Generally Remain in Sound Financial Condition

Passenger traffic and associated revenues have decreased across airports of all sizes, but most airports are still financially sound. Domestic passenger traffic, as measured by enplanements, decreased 4 percent overall in 2008, but by the fourth quarter of 2008, enplanements were down 9 percent compared with the same period in 2007.[36] On average, domestic passenger enplanements decreased between 7 and 12 percent across airport hub sizes in the fourth quarter of 2008, compared with the fourth quarter of 2007, and medium-hub airports experienced the largest percentage decrease in enplanements. (See table 6.) Nevertheless, airport rating agencies indicated that the largest 100 rated commercial service airports are financially sound, especially larger commercial service airports.

Decreases in passenger traffic and airline capacity have reduced airport revenues, impairing the ability of airports to fund both day-to-day operations and future capital improvements. Airport revenue sources from the airlines include landing fees, which are typically based on the number of landings and aircraft weight; terminal rental charges; and fuel-related fees. A large segment of nonairline airport revenue comes from passenger-driven sources such as parking fees; rental payments from retail concessionaires; car rental surcharges; and per-passenger facility charges, which are included in ticketing fees. Based on an industry survey of large- and medium-hub airports, on average, airports earned at least $9 in passenger-based revenue for each enplaned passenger during fiscal year 2007.[37] When revenues are averaged across airports of all sizes, airports draw approximately two-thirds of their total revenue from nonairline sources and the remaining one-third from airline rates and charges. Both types of revenue, however, are very sensitive to changes in passenger traffic. Fewer passengers traveling through an airport can mean less money spent on concessions, car rentals, and parking, and fewer flights can result in less money paid by the airlines to the airport in landing fees. For example, at Oakland International Airport, which experienced a 30 percent decrease in passenger enplanements from 2007 to 2008, food and beverage revenues decreased by 25 percent, and rental car revenues decreased by 20 percent. Officials at Sioux Gateway Airport in Sioux City, Iowa, which experienced a 50 percent decrease in passenger enplanements from 2007 to 2008, project that airport parking revenues will decrease by 24 percent and revenues from airline landing fees will decrease by 47 percent during fiscal year 2008 as a result of Frontier Airlines eliminating service to and from the airport.

With less passenger traffic, airports of all hub sizes will also take in less revenue from PFC collections.[38] Nearly all large-, medium-, and small-hub airports collect PFCs, which they use to fund capital development, both for smaller pay-as-you-go projects and for servicing bonds to finance larger projects. For the first time since the program's inception in

1991, total PFC collections declined during 2008. Specifically, total PFC collections in calendar year 2008 were about $150 million less than total collections in 2007. (See table 7.) Collections in 2009 will depend on how soon passenger traffic rebounds; however, according to an FAA official, current data indicate that PFC collections may continue to decline.

Despite reductions in overall airport revenues, U.S airports in general remain financially sound. According to major credit-rating agencies, the 100 largest rated airports generally have almost 1 year's worth of cash reserves to cover operating expenses (excluding debt service), and some also enjoy the financial backing of state and local governments. While some smaller airports may be more vulnerable to revenue fluctuations, according to airport rating agencies with whom we spoke, the cyclical nature of the airline industry has encouraged airport managers to build cash reserves that are sufficient to support airports through economic downturns.

Table 6. Average Percentage Change in Domestic Enplanements across Airport Hub Sizes, Fourth Quarter 2008 Compared with Fourth Quarter 2007

Airport hub size	Average percentage change in enplanements
Large	-7
Medium	-12
Small	-11
Nonhub	-11

Source: Analysis of DOT T-100 flight data as of December 2008.

Table 7. Total Passenger Facility Charge Collections, by Calendar Year

Calendar year	PFC collections (in millions)
2000	$1,557
2001	1,586
2002	1,857
2003	2,015
2004	2,231[a]
2005	2,448
2006	2,587
2007	2,806[b]
2008	2,660[c]

Source: FAA as of March 2009.

[a]Includes $8,155,034 in corrections to actual collection amounts reported for calendar years 1992 through 2003.

[b]Includes -$18,093,832 in corrections to actual collection amounts reported for calendar years 1992 through 2007.

[c]Includes $3,291,651 in corrections to actual collection amounts reported for calendar years 2005 through 2007.

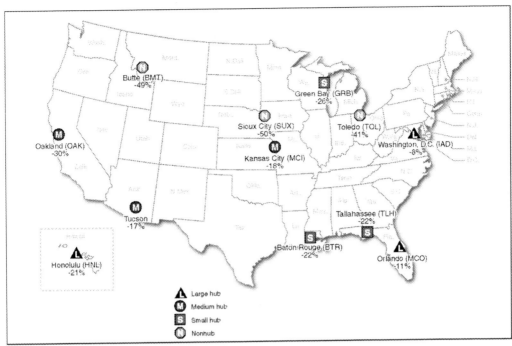

Sources: Analysis of DOT T-100 data; Map Resources (base map).

Figure 7. Change in Passenger Enplanements at 12 Case Study Airports, Fourth Quarter 2007 and Fourth Quarter 2008

In Response to Decreased Revenues, Many Airports Are Reducing Operating Costs, Delaying Capital Improvements, and Diversifying Nonairline Revenue

As revenues from airline and nonairline revenue sources have declined, many airports have taken steps to reduce operating costs, delay capital improvements, and diversify nonairline revenue streams. Our case studies of 12 selected airports illustrate how airports that experienced substantial declines in scheduled airline service during 2008 have responded to declining passenger traffic.[39] Overall, passenger traffic declined between 8 and 50 percent, but the declines varied by airport size at these 12 airports. (See Figure 7.)

To offset reductions in overall revenue, airports have reduced their operating budgets. For instance, Bert Mooney Regional Airport in Butte, Montana, which experienced a 49 percent decline in passenger traffic in 2008, reduced its annual budget by 30 percent, and Austin Straubel International Airport in Green Bay, Wisconsin, which experienced a 26 percent decline in passenger traffic in 2008, reduced its annual budget by 12 percent. (See app. III and IV.) In light of these budget reductions, 11 out of 12 case study airports are reducing operating costs by instituting hiring freezes, laying off staff, or reducing or cutting employee overtime. For instance, at Kansas City International Airport in Kansas City, Missouri, airport management instituted a hiring freeze for nonessential personnel. As a result, approximately 100 of the airport's 550 full-time staff positions were unfilled as of December 2008. Some airports, however, face additional challenges in compensating for revenue decreases. Small and nonhub airports, in particular, may have difficulty responding to decreases in revenue because many airports have relatively fixed operations costs and may therefore lack options for reducing expenditures. For instance, during 2008, Bert Mooney Regional Airport cut its full-time staff by 33 percent, reducing total staff positions from nine to six. Despite these reductions and additional cost-saving efforts to train police and fire staff to fill more than one position, an airport official projects a $120,000 operating budget shortfall for fiscal year 2010. According to this official, the airport could exhaust its cash reserves in late 2009 or early 2010.

In addition to taking steps to reduce operating costs, airports of all sizes are considering options to generate additional revenue, from increasing airline rates and charges to increasing nonairline fees such as parking fees. In addition, airports are diversifying nonairline revenue by developing new revenue sources. For example, airports have begun construction and rental of business parks, sold terminal space for advertising, and instituted fee-based wireless Internet service. In total, 6 of our 12 case study airports have increased nonairline fees in an attempt to raise additional revenue, and 10 of the 12 have taken steps to diversify their nonairline revenue. For example, Tallahassee Regional Airport officials increased airport parking fees by 25 percent during 2008 and recently completed the construction of a service center that will bring in additional revenue from general aviation and cargo traffic.

Many airports are also delaying or canceling scheduled capital improvements. In total, 10 of our 12 case study airports reported delaying or canceling capital improvements for reasons including decreased revenue, less immediate demand for projects intended to expand airport capacity, and problems accessing credit markets. (See table 8 and app. IV).[40] While reductions in capacity and passenger demand have temporarily decreased demand for some projects, such as those related to terminal construction and expansion, other projects remain airport priorities but cannot be completed for lack of available funding. Some delayed projects are fully designed with the necessary environmental approvals and need only funding to begin construction. Airport experts stated that in some cases, delays to capital improvements could leave airports unprepared for future increases in passenger traffic. However, the extent to which airports are delaying capital improvements varies. While some airports have drastically reduced their capital improvement programs, other airports have moved ahead with planned capital improvements. Some airports also indicated that they hoped to compete for the $1.1 billion in discretionary grants that will be awarded to airports under the American Recovery and Reinvestment Act of 2009.[41]

According to airport experts and our case studies, airports vary in their ability to obtain funding for ongoing and planned capital improvement projects. In some cases, unstable financial markets have made it difficult for airports currently completing phased capital improvements to obtain financing to continue construction. For instance, Hartsfield-Jackson International Airport in Atlanta, Georgia, may have to halt a $1.63 billion project to construct a new international terminal because the airport has been unable to sell $600 million in municipal bonds in the face of opposition from a tenant airline. According to an airport official, this airline is concerned that a portion of the costs for additional capital improvements could be passed on to the airline in the form of increased rates and charges. Many airports have also had difficulty obtaining funding from the bond market for future capital improvements. Because of funding constraints, some small and nonhub case study airports reported that they are not pursuing funding from the bond market at all and are instead relying on annual grants, such as those from AIP, to fund projects over an extended time frame, while some larger airports, such as Washington-Dulles International Airport outside Washington, D.C., have turned to short-term financing options, such as commercial paper money market securities, to fund needed improvements. On the other hand, airports that began projects prior to the ongoing economic downturn may be better positioned to complete those projects. For instance, officials from Kansas City International Airport stated that the airport has accelerated some projects to capitalize on low construction costs.

Some Passengers Have Lost Access to Markets, and Some Are Paying Higher Fares

Airline capacity reductions extend across airports of all sizes. From the fourth quarter of 2007 to the fourth quarter of 2008, large hub airports lost 8 percent of domestic scheduled seats, medium hub airports lost 12 percent, small hub airports lost 10 percent, and nonhub airports lost 11 percent. (See Figure 8.) As discussed earlier in this chapter, further capacity reductions are planned for the first half of 2009.

As a result of airline capacity reductions, some passengers have lost some or—in the case of 38 small communities—all scheduled airline service. (See app. V.) From 2007 to 2008, the number of nonstop destinations declined across airports of all sizes. (See table 9.) For example, Little Rock National Airport, a small hub airport in Arkansas, had nonstop flights to 22 cities in the fourth quarter of 2007, but by the fourth quarter of 2008, had lost nonstop service to 6 of its destinations, including nonstop service to large hub airports at Washington-Dulles and Minneapolis, for a net decrease in destinations served by nonstop service of 27 percent. Additionally, Los Angeles International Airport lost nonstop service to 12 of its 92 destinations while gaining nonstop service to 4, for a net decrease in destinations served by nonstop service of 9 percent.

Table 8. Capital Improvement Projects at Case Study Airports Delayed or Canceled

Airport	Project description	Estimated project cost	Project status
Austin Straubel International Airport, Green Bay, Wisconsin	Parking lot and exit road expansion	$2.2 million	Canceled
Oakland International Airport, Oakland, California	Multiple projects including a new terminal building, cargo and pass-enger airline tenant support cen-ters, and pavement rehabilitation	More than $1 billion	Canceled
Bert Mooney Regional Airport, Butte, Montana	Installation of additional runway lighting	$2.5 million	Delayed
	Terminal renovation to increase energy efficiency	$5 million to $7 million	Delayed
Sioux Gateway Airport, Sioux City, Iowa	Terminal renovation	$1.8 million	Delayed
	Runway reconstruction	$12 million	Delayed

Source: Airport officials.

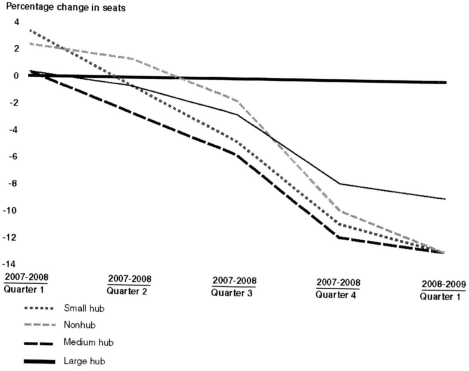

Percentage change in seats

Source: GAO analysis of OAG data.

Note: Seats are based on nonstop, one-way flights.

Figure 8. Percentage Change in Domestic Scheduled Seats by Airport Hub Size (from First Quarter 2007 through First Quarter 2009)

Table 9. Change in the Number of Nonstop Destinations by Airport Hub Size (from Fourth Quarter 2007 to Fourth Quarter 2008)

Airport hub size	Nonstop Destinations 4Q07	Nonstop Destinations 4Q08	Change in number of nonstop destinations	Percentage change
Large	2,810	2,607	-203	-7
Med.	1,400	1,210	-190	-14
Small	1,043	874	-169	-16
Nonhub	950	847	-103	-11

Source: GAO analysis of OAG data.

Note: Results across airport hub sizes cannot be added because some routes between airports of different hub sizes may be double counted.

From the fourth quarter of 2007 to the fourth quarter of 2008, 11 of our 12 case study airports lost nonstop service to between 6 and 63 percent of their nonstop destinations; however, not all of these losses had a significant impact on the ability of passengers to connect to their final destination through airline network hubs.[42] Despite overall reductions in service, 4 of our 12 case study airports did not lose nonstop service to any airline hubs, 3 lost nonstop service to 1 airline hub, and the remaining airports lost nonstop service to 2 to 5 airline hubs. (See app. III for more detailed information on case study airports' route losses.)

For example, from the fourth quarter of 2007 to the fourth quarter of 2008, Kansas City International Airport lost nonstop service to 21 of its 69 total destinations; however, only 1 of these destinations was an airline network hub. For other airports, however, nonstop service to airline hubs has significantly declined. For instance, Baton Rouge Regional Airport lost nonstop service to four of its eight destinations, including losing nonstop service to three airline hubs.[43] (See Figure 9.)

Airline capacity reductions had a particularly significant impact on smaller airports. As airlines adjusted fleet size and reduced domestic capacity, some smaller airports experienced significant shifts in service and many lost scheduled service altogether. From the fourth quarter of 2007 to the fourth quarter of 2008, 38 airports lost all scheduled air service, approximately twice the number of airports that lost scheduled service from the fourth quarter of 2006 to the fourth quarter of 2007. (See app. V.) Additionally, nearly three times fewer airports regained service from the fourth quarter of 2007 and the fourth quarter of 2008, compared with the same periods for 2006 and 2007. Of the 38 airports that lost all scheduled service, 14 were part of the Essential Air Service (EAS) program and were eligible to regain air service with government assistance. (See app. V.) According to DOT, these 14 airports are scheduled to have service restored by May 2009.[44] Additionally, 14 airports that had direct service to two or more markets in 2007 had direct service to only one market during the fourth quarter of 2008. While these airports do not represent a large share of the overall passenger traffic in the United States, officials from some airports and communities affected by the service reductions expressed concern about the impact of service losses and reductions on local businesses and residents.

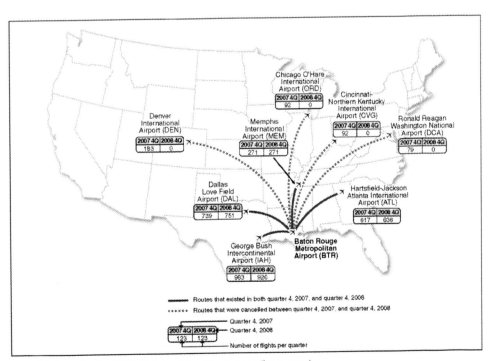

Sources: GAO analysis of OAG data; Map Resources (base map).

Figure 9. Change in Nonstop Scheduled Routes Departing from Baton Rouge Metropolitan Airport (from Fourth Quarter 2007 to Fourth Quarter 2008)

In addition to service losses and reductions, passengers in some communities had fare increases. On average, domestic airfares increased by 18 percent from the third quarter of 2007 to the third quarter of 2008. At airports with capacity reductions of more than 10 percent, fares increased even more, with average airfares increasing by an average of 21 percent during the same time period. Case study airports also experienced fare shifts from the third quarter of 2007 to the third quarter of 2008, ranging from a 7 percent decrease in average fares to a 73 percent increase. In total, 4 of our 12 case study airports experienced airfare increases of more than 30 percent, 6 experienced increases of between 6 and 16 percent, and the remaining 2 airports experienced modest decreases, according to DOT data (see app. III). However, some data indicate that average fares decreased during the fourth quarter of 2008 and the first quarter of 2009. While domestic commercial airfare data were not yet available for these quarters, data from the Air Transport Association show that monthly domestic passenger yields, which represent the average price passengers pay to fly 1 mile (excluding taxes), decreased by 11 percent from October 2008 to January 2009.

Because of the Deteriorating Economy and Declining Passenger Traffic, Lower-than-Anticipated Trust Fund Revenues May Reduce the Trust Fund's Uncommitted Balance in 2009

With the declines in passenger traffic and aircraft operations and reduced fuel consumption, revenues to the Trust Fund are expected to fall significantly below forecasted levels in fiscal year 2009.[45] During fiscal year 2008, domestic passenger traffic (as measured by enplanements) declined 2 percent as compared to fiscal year 2007, whereas FAA had forecast a 1 percent increase. This difference resulted in lower revenues than FAA had forecast in its baseline estimate. Actual revenues of $12.06 billion in fiscal year 2008 were about 4 percent lower than the $12.62 billion in revenues that FAA forecast in its 2008 budget proposal in February 2007. As general economic conditions have continued to deteriorate, FAA officials have said they expect revenues to fall significantly below forecast levels throughout fiscal year 2009.[46] FAA recently forecast a 7.8 percent decrease in domestic passenger traffic for fiscal year 2009. According to FAA and Treasury officials, the Administration is considering transferring the responsibility for revenue forecasts for the Trust Fund to the Treasury Department in an effort to have all federal excise tax forecasts performed by the Treasury.

When actual revenues coming into the Trust Fund are below FAA's forecasted levels, the Trust Fund's uncommitted balance, or surplus, declines. Since the Trust Fund's creation in 1970, revenues have in the aggregate exceeded spending commitments from FAA's appropriations, resulting in a surplus.[47] In recent years, the Trust Fund's uncommitted balance has declined as it has been used to offset lower-than-forecast Trust Fund revenues. As we have previously reported, for each fiscal year beginning with 2001, actual revenues have been less than forecast, so that in each year since then the uncommitted balance has fallen.[48] Since FAA's forecasts are based on information from the first quarter of the preceding fiscal year, its revenue forecasts are inherently uncertain because it is difficult to anticipate future events that may significantly affect the demand for air travel, the fares that passengers pay, and other variables that affect Trust Fund revenues. One of the greatest declines in the uncommitted balance occurred in 2002 following the sudden drop off in aviation activity after the terrorist attacks of September 11, 2001. The Trust Fund's uncommitted balance, which exceeded $7.3 billion at the end of fiscal year 2001, has since dropped to about $1.4 billion at the end of fiscal year 2008. (See Figure 10.) In the fiscal year 2009 omnibus appropriation, Congress increased the General Fund contribution to FAA's operations and decreased FAA's appropriation from the Trust Fund by approximately $1 billion less than what was originally outlined in FAA's fiscal year 2009 budget proposal. According to FAA, this action was in response to the anticipated decline in Trust Fund revenues for fiscal year 2009. Because of this lower appropriation from the Trust Fund, FAA does not expect the uncommitted balance to decrease significantly during fiscal year 2009. However, the Congressional Budget Office recently forecast the uncommitted balance to fall to $752 million.[49] Until actual revenues coming into the Trust Fund for the entire year are known and compared with money appropriated from the Trust Fund, it is difficult to determine the extent to which, if any, the Trust Fund's uncommitted balance will have fallen in fiscal year 2009.

A further decline in the Trust Fund's uncommitted balance could pose budgetary challenges for FAA.[50] If the actual Trust Fund revenues continue to fall below forecasted levels, there could be a risk of overcommitting available resources from the Trust Fund— meaning revenues could be insufficient to cover all of the obligations that FAA has the authority to incur.[51] As the Trust Fund's uncommitted balance approaches zero, this decline signals to FAA that limited revenues are available to incur new obligations while still covering expenditures on existing obligations and increases FAA's challenge in moving forward with planned projects and programs. FAA officials noted that they closely monitor the Trust Fund's available cash and FAA's obligations to ensure enough cash and budget authority are available to cover FAA's expenditures and obligations. In the short term, if there was a risk of overcommitting Trust Fund resources, FAA officials noted that they might be required to delay obligations for capital programs if they do not have adequate revenues in the Trust Fund to cover those obligations—unless additional funding were authorized and appropriated from the General Fund.[52] To reduce the potential impact of future Trust Fund revenue shortfalls and make it less likely that the Trust Fund's uncommitted balance would reach zero, the House of Representatives' current FAA reauthorization bill includes a provision that would limit the budgetary resources made available from the Trust Fund to 90 percent, rather than 100 percent, of forecasted revenues and carry over any remaining positive balance to a subsequent year.[53] Congress would need to provide an additional General Fund contribution in the first 2 years to make up the difference.

In the longer term, future Trust Fund revenues under the current tax structure may be lower than previously anticipated. For example, the Congressional Budget Office is now forecasting about $18 billion less in Trust Fund revenues from 2009 through 2017 than it forecast in 2007 for that same time period. Given the decline in expected future revenues, appropriations from the Trust Fund under current law will be lower in future years than has been expected unless new revenue sources are found. To maintain appropriations consistent with the level that earlier forecasts would have afforded, Congress could take action such as increasing the General Fund contribution or increasing Trust Fund revenues. For example, Congress could generate additional revenue for the Trust Fund by adding airline fees, such as those recently established for checked bags, to the current tax base. Under the governing Internal Revenue Service (IRS) regulations, services beyond those to transport passengers, such as checking baggage, are not included in the tax base for the Trust Fund.[54] Concurrent with the rise in fuel prices in 2008, many airlines instituted new fees for checking first and second bags and for other services, instead of raising fares. To the extent that airlines continue to rely on revenues from baggage fees instead of revenues from higher fares, the Trust Fund will not benefit because the additional fees, under current IRS regulations, do not generate additional ticket tax revenues, whereas higher fares would. Had the $635 million in baggage fees collected by airlines in the first 3 quarters of 2008 been taxed at the same 7.5 percent rate as fares are taxed, an additional $47.6 million in revenue would have been generated for the Trust Fund.[55]

CONCLUSIONS

Since 2001, the U.S. passenger airline industry has experienced substantial losses and numerous bankruptcies and liquidations. The industry struggled to weather financial pressures even before fuel prices rose to historic levels during 2008, forcing many airlines to reduce capacity in order to survive. The current economic downturn and associated declines in passenger demand for air travel have led some airlines to consider additional cuts in capacity for 2009 and have increased concerns about the financial health of some airports and passengers' access to a vibrant aviation system. While passenger demand may recover in the long term, the near-term effects on the financial health of the Trust Fund may warrant congressional response.

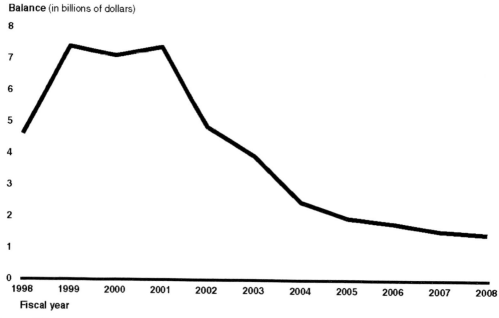

Source: FAA.

Figure 10. Airport and Airway Trust Fund End-of-Year Uncommitted Balance, Fiscal Years 1999 through 2008

Volatile fuel prices, the economic downturn, and the airlines' response to these pressures have, in turn, affected others: airports, communities, passengers, and the Trust Fund. Airports are generally better able to withstand a downturn in air travel than airlines, but at some airports, passenger traffic has taken a more significant downturn, and some of these airports are struggling to adjust quickly enough. In addition, some communities and passengers are losing service and facing higher fares—a trend that may continue. Finally, although FAA received additional General Fund money in its fiscal year 2009 appropriation to offset lower-than-anticipated Trust Fund revenues,[56] the Trust Fund's uncommitted balance could potentially fall close to zero in the near future, since revenues coming into the Trust Fund have consistently fallen short of forecasts. A further decline in the uncommitted balance toward zero warns FAA that funds may not be available to start or continue some projects for which appropriations have been made. The declining uncommitted balance also signals to Congress that it may need to make some difficult choices about whether to reduce FAA's appropriations or to take actions to either increase revenues going into the Trust Fund or increase appropriations from the General Fund for FAA.

MATTER FOR CONGRESSIONAL CONSIDERATION

Given the inherent uncertainty of forecasting revenues and the deteriorating uncommitted balance of the Trust Fund, Congress should consider working with FAA to develop alternative ways to reduce the risk of overcommitting budgetary resources from the Trust Fund. Better matching of actual revenues to the appropriation from the Trust Fund would help to ensure sufficient Trust Fund revenues are available to cover all the obligations that FAA has the authority to incur, thus reducing the risk of disruptions in funding for aviation projects and programs. One approach would be to appropriate less than 100 percent of the forecasted revenues, especially until a sufficient surplus is established to protect against potential disruptions in revenue collection. This change would reduce the likelihood that FAA would incur obligations in excess of the cash needed to liquidate these obligations and thus reduce the risk of delaying or terminating projects. Another approach would be to target a minimum level for the Trust Fund's uncommitted balance and base appropriations on the goal of maintaining that target level. This change would make it more likely that uncommitted resources would be available to FAA in the event that actual revenues fell short of forecasted revenues in a future year. Either approach would result in fewer available resources for some period of time, unless a General Fund contribution made up the difference.

APPENDIX I. SCOPE AND METHODOLOGY

To determine how the financial condition of the U.S. passenger airline industry has changed, the principal factors affecting its condition, and its future prospects, we analyzed financial and operational data, reviewed relevant studies, and interviewed industry experts. We analyzed the Department of Transportation's (DOT) Form 41 financial and operational data submitted to DOT by airlines from the years 1990 through the third quarter of 2008—the most recent and complete data available. We obtained these data from BACK Aviation

Solutions, a private contractor that provides online access to U.S. airline financial, operational, and passenger data with a query-based user interface. All dollar figures in this chapter are nominal unless otherwise noted. To assess the reliability of these data as well as DOT's T-100 enplanement data and origin and destination (OD1B) data and the Official Airline Guide (OAG) schedule data, we reviewed the quality control procedures used by BACK Aviation and DOT and subsequently determined that the data were sufficiently reliable for our purposes. The data for the fourth quarter of 2008 represent the 11 largest airlines that report to the Securities and Exchange Commission (SEC), including Alaska Airlines, American Airlines, Continental Airlines, Delta Air Lines, United Airlines, US Airways, AirTran Airways, Frontier Airlines, JetBlue Airways, Southwest Airlines, and Hawaiian Airlines, since data for all U.S. passenger airlines were not yet available from DOT. In the first 3 quarters of 2008, these airlines' operating revenues represented 75 percent of U.S. domestic passenger airline revenues and, therefore, provide a good indication of the overall financial status of the industry in the fourth quarter of 2008. Although the airlines' SEC filings include audited financial data, we also compared financial data from airlines' previous SEC filings with historical data from BACK Aviation and determined that the data were sufficiently reliable for our purposes. We also reviewed government and expert data analyses, research, and studies, as well as our own previous studies. The expert research and studies, where applicable, were reviewed by a GAO economist or were corroborated with additional sources to determine that they were sufficiently reliable for our purposes. Finally, we conducted interviews with DOT and Federal Aviation Administration (FAA) officials, airlines and their trade associations, credit and equity analysts, labor representatives, industry experts, and academics. The analysts, experts, and academics were identified and selected based on literature review, prior GAO work, and recommendations from within the industry.

To identify how airlines have responded to factors affecting their financial condition, we interviewed airline managers, trade association representatives, and industry experts. We analyzed OAG schedule data to determine the airlines' changes in domestic capacity and fleet mix. We also reviewed the airlines' SEC filings to identify the total number of active fleet for the U.S. passenger airline industry. We analyzed DOT data on airline employment to determine changes in employee levels. To assess the airlines' fees, we reviewed company reports and analyzed DOT Form 41 data.

To assess how changes in the U.S. passenger airline industry have affected airports, passengers, and the Airport and Airway Trust Fund (Trust Fund), we analyzed DOT data on enplanements and OAG data on airline schedules; spoke with airport consultants, FAA officials, and industry associations; and conducted 12 case studies of large, medium, small, and nonhub airports from different regions of the United States. These case studies allowed us to assess airport actions in response to airline service reductions, including changes to capital improvement plans, operating budgets, and rates and changes. We selected our case study airports on the basis of three characteristics: hub size, geographic diversity, and overall degree of service reduction. All case study airports selected were among the 10 airports within their hub size to experience the greatest domestic capacity reductions, as measured by changes in numbers of scheduled seats when comparing the third quarter of 2007 with the third quarter of 2008. Among the airports that experienced the greatest domestic capacity reductions, three airports from each hub size were selected as case study airports based on geographic distribution throughout the United States. Case study airports do not constitute a representative sample of U.S. airports and information collected from case study airports is not generalizable to other U.S. airports. To assess how changes in the passenger airline industry have affected passengers, we analyzed DOT data on fares and OAG data on airline schedules. Our assessment of change in average fares from the third quarter of 2007 to the third quarter of 2008 included an assessment of change in average stage length to ensure that fare changes were not attributable to changes in stage length.[57] To assess the effect on the Trust Fund, we interviewed FAA officials and reviewed DOT data on the Trust Fund, relevant legislation, and prior GAO reports.

We conducted this performance audit from July 2008 to April 2009 in accordance with generally accepted government auditing standards. Those standards require that we plan and perform the audit to obtain sufficient, appropriate evidence to provide a reasonable basis for our findings and conclusions based on our audit objectives. We believe that the evidence obtained provides a reasonable basis for our findings and conclusions based on our audit objectives.

APPENDIX II. U.S. PASSENGER AIRLINE LABOR CONTRACTS AND THEIR AMENDABLE DATES

Airline	Pilots	Flight attendants	Mechanics & related	Dispatchers	Agents
AirTran	4/1/05	11/30/08	10/1/09 (Mechanics) 8/31/11 (GSE) 6/1/11 (Stock)	12/31/08	Nonunion
Air Wisconsin	10/1/11	10/1/08	8/1/08	1/2/12	1/29/12
Alaska	5/1/07 TA reached 3/09	5/1/12	10/16/09 (Mechanics) 7/19/10 (Stock/ramp)	6/30/10	7/19/10
American	4/30/08	4/30/08	4/30/08 (Mechanics and ramp)	4/30/08	Nonunion
American Eagle	10/31/13	10/27/09	10/2/07	1/27/08	1/23/08
Atlantic Southeast	11/21/10	7/21/11	Nonunion	4/19/06	Nonunion
Cape Air	Initial mediation	Nonunion	Nonunion	Nonunion	Nonunion
Colgan Air	Initial negotiations	4/30/14	Nonunion	Nonunion	Nonunion
Comair	3/1/11	12/31/10	12/31/10	Nonunion	Nonunion
CommutAir	Initial negotiations	Initial negotiations	Nonunion	Nonunion	Nonunion
Compass	4/1/13	Nonunion	Nonunion	Nonunion	Nonunion
Continental	1/1/09	12/31/09	12/31/08	12/31/08	Nonunion
Delta, including Northwest	12/31/12 (Delta and Northwest)	Nonunion (Delta) 12/31/11 (Northwest)	Nonunion (Delta) 12/31 /1 1 (Mechanics—Northwest) 12/31/10 (Stock/ramp—Northwest)	12/31/13 (Delta) 12/31/11 (Northwest)	Nonunion (Delta)12/31/10 (Northwest)
ExpressJet	11/30/10	7/31/10	8/1/09	7/7/09	Nonunion

Table. (Continued)

Airline	Pilots	Flight attendants	Mechanics & related	Dispatchers	Agents
Frontier	3/2/12	Nonunion	10/31/11 (Mechanics) 9/16/15 (Cleaner) 10/31/11 (Stock)	9/15/12	Nonunion
GoJet	1/19/13	Nonunion	Nonunion	Nonunion	Nonunion
Great Lakes	**9/16/09**	**3/31/03**	**11/1/05** **4/1/02 (Stock)**	**Initial negotiations**	Nonunion
Gulfstream	**7/1/09**	Initial mediation	Nonunion	Nonunion	Nonunion
Hawaiian	6/30/07	10/31/07 TA reached 2/09	3/31/08	11/30/07	3/31/08 TA reached 3/09
Horizon	**9/13/06**	**11/21/07**	**11/30/08**	10/6/08	Nonunion
IslandAir	**11/30/07**	**7/31/07**	**11/4/06** **8/31/08 (Stock)**	**9/30/08**	**7/31/07**
Mesa	11/2010	**6/13/06**	Nonunion	Nonunion	Nonunion
Mesaba	6/1/12	6/1/12	6/1/12	6/1/12	Nonunion
Midwest	**8/31/08**	**7/24/08**	Nonunion	Nonunion	Nonunion
Piedmont (Merged with Allegheny)	**5/17/09**	**8/31/09**	**2/25/09 (Piedmont)** 2/3/10 (Allegheny) **Mediation for combined collective bargaining agreement Initial negotiations (Stock)**	**2/24/09**	Nonunion
Pinnacle	**4/30/05**	1/31/11	Nonunion	1/1/14	3/18/10
PSA	**7/1/09**	**8/31/09**	**9/24/09**	**Initial Mediation**	12/15/10
Republic / Chautauqua / Shuttle America	10/17/07	9/1/09	Nonunion	6/2/12 (Chautauqua only)	11/19/12 (Chautauqua only)
SkyWest	Nonunion	Nonunion	Nonunion	Nonunion	Nonunion
Spirit	1/31/07	8/6/07	Nonunion	7/26/12	Nonunion
Southwest	8/31/06 TA reached 3/09	5/31/08 TA reached 3/09	8/16/12 (Mechanics) **8/16/08 (Stock)** **2/16/09 (Cleaner)**	**11/30/09**	**10/31/08 (CSA)** 6/30/11 (Ramp)
Trans States	8/1/06	2/20/13	Nonunion	Nonunion	Nonunion
United	**12/31/09**	1/7/10	**12/31/09 (Mechanics)** **12/31/09 (Stock/ramp)**	1/1/10	**12/31/09**
US Airways[a]	**12/31/09 (US Airways)** **12/30/06 (America West)**	12/31/11 (US Airways) **5/4/04 (America West)**	12/31/11	**12/31/09**	1/1/12 (CSA) 12/31/11 (Ramp)

Source: F&H Solutions Group.

Note: The contracts in bold represent those that are amendable on or before December 31, 2009. Labor classifications include Customer Service Agent (CSA); Ramp Worker (Ramp); Stock and Supply Worker (Stock); Aircraft housekeeping (Cleaner); Aircraft Mechanics (Mechanics); Ground Support Equipment Personnel (GSE). Nonunion means that no labor union represents the particular work group at that airline. Also, "TA reached" means that the airline and union have reached a tentative agreement on month and year mentioned in the table.

[a]Since the merger, US Airways has been in the process of integrating labor agreements between US Airways and America West Airlines between the pilots and the flight attendants.

APPENDIX III. IMPACT OF U.S. PASSENGER AIRLINE INDUSTRY CONTRACTION ON CASE STUDY AIRPORTS

Airport	Change in enplanements (4Q07 to 4Q08)[a]	Change in capacity – total scheduled seats (4Q07 to 4Q08)[b]	Markets served (nonstop)[c]				Change in airfares[d]		
			4Q07	4Q08	Percentage change[e]	Hubs lost	3Q07	3Q08	Percent change
Dulles (IAD)	-8%	-11%	83	83	0	0	$199	$224	12
Honolulu (HNL)	-21%	-19%	32	30	-6	0	137	180	32
Orlando (MCO)	-11%	-13%	85	72	-15	0	124	141	13
Kansas City (MCI)	-18%	-19%	69	48	-30	1	139	160	16
Oakland (OAK)	-30%	-26%	37	26	-30	5	126	134	6
Tucson (TUS)	-17%	-14%	28	18	-36	2[f]	128	142	11
Baton Rouge (BTR)	-22%	-23%	8	4	-50	3	194	193	-1
Green Bay (GRB)	-26%	-19%	11	8	-27	3	188	261	38
Tallahassee (TLH)	-22%	-28%	9	7	-22	1	229	214	-7
Butte (BTM)	-49%	-61%	2	1	-50	0	193	214	11
Sioux City (SUX)	-50%	-45%	2	1	-50	1	268	356	33
Toledo (TOL)	-41%	-54%	8	3	-63	3	117	204	73

Source: GAO analysis of DOT data.

[a]GAO analysis of DOT T-100 data as of December 2008.

[b]GAO analysis of OAG data as of December 2008.

[c]GAO analysis of OAG data as of December 2008.

[d]GAO analysis of DOT OD1B as of September 2008

[e]Calculation of percentage change in fares is based on fare data to two decimal places.

[f]Tucson Airport also gained service to one airline hub from fourth quarter 2007 to fourth quarter 2008.

APPENDIX IV. AIRPORT ACTIONS IN RESPONSE TO U.S. PASSENGER AIRLINE INDUSTRY CONTRACTION

Airport	Hub size	Lease type		Overall budget change	Airport actions						
		Airside	Landside		Delay or cancel capital projects	Hiring freeze	Staff lay-offs	Other, staff related[a]	Increase airline fees	Increase non-Airline fees[b]	Plans to diversify non-airline revenue
Dulles (IAD)	Large	Compensatory	Compensatory	+0.8%	√			√		√	√
Honolulu (HNL)	Large	Residual	Residual	-10.0%	√	√		√	√	√	√
Orlando (MCO)	Large	Hybrid	Hybrid	0.0	√	√		√		√	√

Table. (Continued)

Airport	Hub size	Lease type		Overall budget change	Airport actions						
		Airside	Landside		Delay or cancel capital projects	Hiring freeze	Staff lay-offs	Other, staff related[a]	Increase airline fees	Increase non-Airline fees[b]	Plans to diversify non-airline revenue
Kansas City (MCI)	Medium	Residual	Compensatory	-6.3%		√		√			√
Oakland (OAK)	Medium	Residual	Hybrid	-5.5%	√						
Tucson (TUS)	Medium	Residual	Residual	-0.4%	√			√			√
Baton Rouge (BTR)	Small	Hybrid	Hybrid	0.0		√		√			√
Green Bay (GRB)	Small	Hybrid	Hybrid	-11.6%	√		√			√	√
Tallahassee (TLH)	Small	Hybrid	Hybrid	c	√	√			√	√	√
Butte (BTM)	Non-hub	Hybrid	Hybrid	-30.0%	√				√	√	
Sioux City (SUX)	Non-hub	Hybrid	Compensatory	-5.0%	√					√	√
Toledo (TOL)	Non-hub	Compensatory	Hybrid	-12.5%	√	√		√			√

Source: Airport officials.

Notes: Compensatory lease: The airport operator assumes the major financial risk of running the airport and sets rates and charges to recover the costs of the facilities and services that the airlines use.

Residual lease: The airlines collectively assume significant financial risk by agreeing to pay any costs of running the airport that not allocated to other users or covered by nonairline revenue.

Hybrid lease combines certain elements compensatory and residual lease agreements. Landside lease includes area of the airport such as terminals and airport access. Airside lease includes areas of the airport such as runways and taxiways.

[a]Includes reductions to training and travel budgets, pay freezes, and reductions to overtime hours.

[b]Includes parking fees, car rental surcharges, and non-airline rents.

[c]Budget reduction to be determined.

APPENDIX V. U.S. AIRPORTS WITH LOSS OF ALL COMMERCIAL SERVICE FROM FOURTH QUARTER 2007 TO FOURTH QUARTER 2008

	Airport
1.	Bridgeport, Conn.
2.	Bedford/Hanscom, Mass.
3.	Brookings, S. Dak.
4.	Boulder City, Nev.
5.	Bluefield, W.V.

Table. (Continued)

	Airport
6.	Cape Newenham, Alaska
7.	El Dorado, Ariz.[b]
8.	Wildman Lake, Alaska
9.	Excursion Inlet, Alaska[a]
10.	Grand Canyon, Ariz.
11.	Grand Canyon West, Ariz.
12.	Glendive, Mont.[a]
13.	Glasgow, Mont.[a]
14.	Grand Island, Neb.[a]
15.	Gallup, N. Mex.
16.	Hot Spring, Ark.[b]
17.	Harrison, Ark.[b]
18.	Havre, Mont.[a]
19.	Kingman, Ariz.[a]
20.	Kirksville, Mo.[a]
21.	Kinston, N.C.
22.	Jonesboro, Ark.[b]
23.	Sandy River, Alaska
24.	Lopez Island, Wash.
25.	Tampa (MacDill Air Force Base), Fla.
26.	Jackson, Tenn.[b]
27.	Wolf Point, Mont.[a]
28.	Owensboro, Ky.[b]
29.	Portage Creek, Alaska
30.	Portsmouth, N.H.
31.	Roche Harbor, Wash.
32.	Rosario, Wash.
33.	Santa Fe, N. Mex.
34.	Pinehurst, N.C.
35.	Philadelphia, N.J.
36.	Blue Mountain, Alaska
37.	Westsound, Wash.
38.	Youngstown, Ohio

Source: GAO Analysis of OAG data.

[a]Airport participating in the Essential Air Service (EAS) program with service restored as of February 2009.

[b]Airport participating in EAS without service as of February 2009. Service scheduled to be restored in May 2009.

End Notes

[1] With the exception of fourth quarter 2008 data, the airline financial data represent all reporting U.S. domestic passenger airlines, including legacy, low-cost, regional, and other carriers. The fourth quarter data represent 11

airlines that report to the Securities and Exchange Commission (SEC), including Alaska Airlines, American Airlines, Continental Airlines, Delta Air Lines, United Airlines, US Airways, AirTran Airways, Frontier Airlines, JetBlue Airways, Southwest Airlines, and Hawaiian Airlines, since data for all U.S. passenger airlines were not yet available from DOT. In the first 3 quarters of 2008, these airlines' operating revenues represented about 75 percent of U.S. passenger airline operating revenues, and therefore provide a good indication of the overall financial status of the industry in the fourth quarter of 2008. In 2008, Delta and Northwest merged, and the fourth quarter 2008 data for the merged company were filed under Delta.

[2] BACK Aviation Solutions is a private contractor that provides online access to U.S. airline financial, operational, and passenger data with a query-based user interface.

[3] The airports we selected as case studies were among the 10 airports within their hub size that experienced the largest domestic capacity reductions, as measured by changes in the number of scheduled seats from the third quarter of 2007 to the third quarter of 2008.

[4] Regional airlines that are owned by a legacy airline report their financial and operating data with their parent company.

[5] Commercial service airports are defined by 49 U.S.C. § 47102 as having scheduled service and enplaning 2,500 or more passengers each year.

[6] Based on FAA's classification of commercial service airports, nonhub airports enplane fewer than 0.05 percent of systemwide passengers, small hub airports enplane at least 0.05 percent but fewer than 0.25 percent of systemwide passengers, medium hub airports enplane at least 0.25 percent but fewer than 1 percent of systemwide passengers, and large hub airports enplane at least 1 percent of systemwide passengers. *See* 49 U.S.C. § 47102.

[7] GAO, *Airport Finance: Observations on Planned Airport Development Costs and Funding Levels and the Administration's Proposed Changes in the Airport Improvement Program*, GAO-07-885 (Washington, D.C.: June 27, 2007).

[8] Statutorily, large and medium hub airports are designated as primary airports and must contribute a larger share to projects funded under AIP as well as forgo a portion of their AIP entitlement funds if they collect PFCs. *See* 49 U.S.C. § 47114(f).

[9] The excise taxes are related to passenger tickets, passenger flight segments, international arrivals/departures, cargo waybills, and commercial and general aviation fuels. The other source of Trust Fund revenue is interest earned on the Trust Fund balance.

[10] Pub. L. No. 106-181, 114 Stat. 61 (2000).

[11] Pub. L. No. 108-176, 117 Stat. 2490 (2003).

[12] The airlines' losses reported to the SEC may differ from the losses reported to DOT because of different reporting requirements.

[13] The events of September 11 marked a significant decline in domestic passenger revenue as a percentage of the U.S. gross domestic product. One analyst estimates that the gap between the pre-September 11 demand and the post-September 11 demand resulted in $26 billion in lost revenue in 2008 and $150 billion in cumulative lost revenue over the last 7 years.

[14] In 2008, Air Midwest, Aloha Airlines, ATA Airlines, Champion Air, EOS Airlines, Big Sky Air, and Skybus Airlines ceased operation, while Frontier and Sun Country filed for Chapter 11 bankruptcy but are still operating.

[15] For example, Alaska Airlines' pretax income increased to $87.3 million during the second quarter of 2008 from $80.9 million in the second quarter of 2007, as Alaska recorded gains on the market value of its fuel hedges. These gains offset the $129.7 million, or nearly 66 percent, increase in Alaska's fuel costs over the second quarter of 2007.

[16] For example, United Airlines lost more than $1.1 billion in 2008 related to fuel hedge losses. In 2008, US Airways reported $496 million of unrealized losses from mark-to-market adjustments on its fuel hedges. Southwest's average fuel cost per gallon, including hedging, increased 35.6 percent in 2008 and contributed to a $342 million, or 43.2 percent, decrease in the company's operating income; it also lowered the company's cash balance from $5.8 billion in the second quarter of 2008 to $1.8 billion at the end of 2008, its lowest level since 2006.

[17] For example, Southwest Airlines had significantly reduced its hedges from 70 percent previously.

[18] Because of the seasonal nature of the airline industry, financial and operating results are generally compared for the same time periods in each year.

[19] Although data are not yet available for the entire industry, operating revenues are expected to grow in the fourth quarter of 2008. The 11 airlines that comprised about 75 percent of the industry's total operating revenues in the first 3 quarters of 2008 reported about a 6 percent year-over-year growth in operating revenues from the fourth quarter of 2008 compared to the fourth quarter of 2007.

[20] Revenue passenger miles are the number of miles revenue paying passengers are transported and are a measure of passenger traffic.

[21] For advance frequent flyer mileage sales, the credit card company holding the airline's frequent flyer credit card enters into an agreement to provide an advance payment for frequent flyer miles that the credit card company anticipates awarding in the future.

[22] Current forecasts by IHS Global Insight, a leading economic forecasting firm, predict that the U.S. economy will continue to contract during the first 3 quarters of 2009, but the economy is expected to begin recovering in the fourth quarter of 2009.

[23] Airline labor contracts are governed under the Railway Labor Act. *See* 45 U.S.C. § 151, *et seq.* Under this act, airline labor contracts do not expire; rather, they reach an amendable date—the first day that the parties can be required to negotiate the terms of a new contract. Labor negotiations may begin before or after the amendable date, however. While a new contract is being negotiated, the terms of the existing contract remain in effect. Also, the extent of unionization among the major carriers varies significantly (see app. II).

[24] Under the Railway Labor Act, labor negotiations include a series of steps—which may include mediation, arbitration, and presidential interventions—specifically designed to avoid an impasse that would interrupt the flow of essential commerce. After exchanging proposed changes to contract provisions, the airline and the union engage in direct bargaining. If they cannot come to an agreement, the parties must request mediation assistance from NMB. By statute, if NMB is sought to mediate a dispute, it must make its best effort to bring the parties to an amicable settlement. If an amicable settlement cannot be reached by mediation, the controversy may be submitted to arbitration. *See* 45 U.S.C. § 151, *et seq.*

[25] The airlines with defined benefit plans include American Airlines, Continental Airlines, Alaska Air, Hawaiian Airlines, and Delta Airlines along with recently acquired Northwest Airlines. Some of these airlines have "frozen" plans, meaning some or all future pension accruals are limited for some or all plan participants. Depending on the type of freeze, assets and liabilities (and, therefore, the plan's funded status) can change. US Airways and United's plans along with Delta's pilot plan were terminated and the remaining assets and benefit obligations were assumed by Pension Benefit Guaranty Corporation.

[26] In the Pension Protection Act of 2006 (PPA), Pub. L. No. 109-280, Sec. 402, 120 Stat. 922, commercial airlines were given the option to amortize over 10 years (rather than seven) or amortize under an "alternative funding schedule," a 17-year amortization with specific requirements and restrictions. In determining contribution and amortization, the airlines were required to value assets at their fair market value under the PPA. However, the Worker, Retiree, and Employer Recovery Act of 2008 (WRERA), Pub. L. No. 110-458, Sec. 126, 122 Stat. 5116, relaxed this requirement under the "alternative funding schedule," allowing valuation of assets by either a fair market value determination or by averaging fair market values as set forth in 26 U.S.C. § 430(g)(3)(B), the latter of which is used for single-employer defined benefit pension plans.

[27] Because of the seasonal nature of the airline industry, financial and operating results are generally compared for the same time periods in each year.

[28] We categorized airlines into three groups based on prior GAO reports. The seven legacy airlines are Alaska, American, Continental, Delta, Northwest, United, and US Airways, and the six low cost airlines are AirTran, ATA, Frontier, Jet Blue, Southwest, and Spirit. The eight "other" airlines include Allegiant, Aloha, Expressjet, Hawaiian, Midwest, Sun Country and Virgin America. Schedule changes for regional carriers that provide service under code-sharing agreements with legacy carriers are captured in the legacy carriers' schedules.

[29] The data on the total number of active aircraft fleet are based on filings with SEC by American Airlines, Alaska Airlines, AirTran Airways, Continental Airlines, Delta Air Lines, Frontier Airlines, JetBlue Airways, Southwest Airlines, United Airlines, and US Airways. Spirit Airlines fleet information was obtained from the company's Web site.

[30] The total seat reduction is also comprised of 9 percent from regional jets, 5 percent from widebody aircraft, and 3 percent from turboprop aircraft.

[31] A Boeing machinist strike in 2008 will also delay the delivery of some aircraft.

[32] The employee reductions were calculated based on year-over-year changes in the fourth quarter.

[33] Many of these reductions may come via voluntary job-reduction programs.

[34] The earnings listed under other revenues vary by airline and can also include frequent flyer program revenue, flight change and reservation ticketing service charges, revenue from aircraft maintenance and staffing services to third parties, and commissions earned on tickets sold for other airlines and sales of tour packages. Also, some airlines report checked baggage fees as part of "other revenues;" others report checked baggage fees as part of passenger revenues.

[35] The revenues for excess baggage include all U.S. passenger airlines. Fees from first and second bags are reported in data on in excess baggage in DOT Form 41 data.

[36] Enplanements are measured by the total number of passengers boarding a flight, including connecting passengers.

[37] This estimate is based on a survey sample comprising 72 U.S. airports, including 90 percent of large hub airports and 57 percent of medium-hub airports. See Airports Council International, *North American 2008 Benchmarking Survey (FY 2007)*, ACI World/North America Conference & Exhibition, Finance Seminar, September 21, 2008. The revenues represent concessions, parking, ground transportation, and car rental fees and surcharges.

[38] PFCs are a per-passenger charge of up to a statutory maximum of $4.50 that is levied by individual airports to fund FAA-approved projects that enhance safety, security, or capacity; reduce noise; or increase air carrier competition. 49 U.S.C. § 40117(b)(4).

[39] We selected our case study airports on the basis of three characteristics: hub size, geographic diversity, and overall degree of service reduction. All case study airports selected were among the 10 airports within their hub size to experience the greatest domestic capacity reductions, as measured by changes in numbers of scheduled seats, from the third quarter of 2007 to the third quarter of 2008. Case study airports do not constitute a representative sample of U.S. airports and information collected from case study airports is not generalizable to other U.S. airports.

[40] Capital improvement delays and cancellations cited by case study airport officials ranged from 1 to 2 years to indefinite project deferrals.

[41] Pub. L. No. 111-5, 123 Stat. 115, Title XII (2009).

[42] We are defining airline network hub in terms of how airlines utilize airports to distribute passengers within their service network, which is different than FAA's definition of an airport hub used elsewhere in this chapter.

[43] According to DOT and an airport official, Baton Rouge Metropolitan Airport experienced service increases following Hurricane Katrina in 2005. Some service losses at Baton Rouge Metropolitan Airport may be attributed to service returning to New Orleans International Airport.

[44] The EAS program was established in 1978 to ensure that small communities served by commercial air service prior to deregulation would maintain at least a minimal level of scheduled air service. DOT currently subsidizes commuter airline service to approximately 140 rural communities across the country.

[45] Some of the decline in Trust Fund revenues could also be attributed to a decline in tax revenues from cargo and general aviation.

[46] FAA updates its revenues forecasts for the next fiscal year in a mid-session review. According to an FAA official, this update is provided to the appropriations committees and can be used in the appropriations process, depending on the status of the appropriations bills. The next revenue forecast will be provided as part of the President's Budget for fiscal year 2010.

[47] FAA considers annual appropriations from the Trust Fund as part of its committed balance—that is, these funds are committed for specific purposes but have not yet been liquidated through outlays. The committed balance consists of both obligated and unobligated amounts. The uncommitted balance represents the revenues in the Trust Fund that have not yet been appropriated or authorized with contract authority.

[48] GAO, *Federal Aviation Administration: An Analysis of the Financial Viability of the Airport and Airway Trust Fund*, GAO-06-562T (Washington, D.C.: Mar. 28, 2006).

[49] According to FAA, a revised estimate for the Trust Fund's uncommitted balance and revenues for fiscal year 2009 will be published with the upcoming fiscal year 2010 President's budget details expected to be released in early May.

[50] We have identified the funding of the nation's surface transportation system on our high-risk list because of the federal, state, and local governments' challenges in providing funds to maintain and expand the nation's surface transportation system. See GAO, *High-Risk Series: An Update*, GAO-09-271 (Washington, D.C.: January 2009).

[51] An obligation is an action that creates a legal liability or definite commitment on the part of the government to make a disbursement at some later date. FAA's fiscal year appropriations and authorization provide the legal authority for FAA to incur obligations and make payments out of the Trust Fund (through the Treasury).

[52] According to FAA officials, they would start by deferring or deobligating some existing obligations related to FAA's capital programs to continue to first fund operating expenses, such as air traffic control and safety inspections. These actions would ensure that the agency did not incur obligations in excess of the Trust Fund's cash balance, which could potentially lead to a violation of the Antideficiency Act. This act prohibits an officer or employee of the federal government from incurring an obligation, or making an expenditure, in advance or in excess of an appropriation or fund. 31 U.S.C. § 1341(a)(1). However, FAA's aviation programs are partly funded with contract authority, which is an exemption to the Antideficiency Act and authorizes FAA to incur obligations in advance or in excess of an appropriation. This authority permits FAA to incur obligations in excess of the revenue in the Trust Fund. However, FAA must receive an appropriation from the Trust Fund in order to liquidate these obligations. If there is not adequate revenue in the Trust Fund, the obligation cannot be liquidated. Because of the uncertainty in forecasting, the addition of revenues into the Trust Fund throughout the fiscal year, and the mix of FAA programs funded through contract authority and through regular appropriations, it may be difficult for FAA to determine at what point it would violate the Antideficiency Act. Accordingly, FAA must carefully manage its obligations and expenditures so that it can take action before it reaches the point where it could potentially incur an Antideficiency Act violation.

[53] This provision is contained in H.R. 915, 111th Cong. (2009), introduced on February 9, 2009, but was amended from 95 percent to 90 percent on March 5, 2009. H.R. 2881, 110th Cong. (2007), which was introduced last session, passed in the House on September 20, 2007, and included a provision to limit FAA's budget authority to 95 percent.

[54] These regulations (26 C.F.R. §§ 49.4261-7, 49.4261-8 (2008)) were promulgated in 1959 (24 Fed. Reg. 9668 (Dec. 3, 1959)) under authority provided in 26 U.S.C. § 7805. The regulations were amended in 1962 (27 Fed. Reg. 11223 (Nov. 14, 1962)) and have not been amended since that time.

[55] As previously mentioned, the airlines' fees for checked baggage can be included in other revenues; however, some of the airlines' other revenues, including revenue from flight change fees, are taxed. In addition to the checked baggage fees, the recently instituted fees collected for other items, such as meals and beverages, are not subject to any tax, but these amounts are small compared with the revenues generated from checked baggage.

[56] Omnibus Appropriations Act of 2009, Pub. L. No. 111-8, 123 Stat. 524, Sec. 104 (2009).

[57] Average stage length, as weighted by the number of passengers, did not change significantly from the third quarter of 2007 to the third quarter of 2008.

In: Airline Industry Mergers: Background and Issues
Editor: Felix J. Mercado

ISBN: 978-1-61761-993-9
© 2011 Nova Science Publishers, Inc.

Chapter 9

AIRLINE INDUSTRY: POTENTIAL MERGERS AND ACQUISITIONS DRIVEN BY FINANCIAL AND COMPETITIVE PRESSURES

United States Government Accountability Office

WHY GAO DID THIS STUDY

The airline industry is vital to the U.S. economy, generating operating revenues of nearly $172 billion in 2007, amounting to over 1 percent of the U.S. gross domestic product. It serves as an important engine for economic growth and a critical link in the nation's transportation infrastructure, carrying more than 700 million passengers in 2007. Airline deregulation in 1978, led, at least in part, to increasingly volatile airline profitability, resulting in periods of significant losses and bankruptcies. In response, some airlines have proposed or are considering merging with or acquiring another airline.

GAO was asked to help prepare Congress for possible airline mergers or acquisitions. This chapter describes (1) the financial condition of the U.S. passenger airline industry, (2) whether the industry is becoming more or less competitive, (3) why airlines seek to merge with or acquire other airlines, and (4) the role of federal authorities in reviewing proposed airline mergers and acquisitions. To answer these objectives, we analyzed Department of Transportation (DOT) financial and operating data; interviewed agency officials, airline managers, and industry experts; and reviewed *Horizontal Merger Guidelines* and spoke with antitrust experts.

DOT and the Department of Justice (DOJ) provided technical comments, which were incorporated as appropriate.

WHAT GAO FOUND

The U.S. passenger airline industry was profitable in 2006 and 2007 for the first time since 2000, but this recovery appears short-lived because of rapidly increasing fuel costs. Legacy airlines (airlines that predate deregulation in 1978) generally returned to modest profitability in 2006 and 2007 by reducing domestic capacity, focusing on more profitable markets, and reducing long-term debt. Low-cost airlines (airlines that entered after deregulation), meanwhile, continued to be profitable. Airlines, particularly legacy airlines, were also able to reduce costs, especially through bankruptcy- and near-bankruptcy-related employee contract, pay, and pension plan changes. Recent industry forecasts indicate that the industry is likely to incur substantial losses in 2008 owing to high fuel prices.

Competition within the U.S. domestic airline industry increased from 1998 through 2006, as reflected by an increase in the number of competitors in city-to-city (city-pair) markets, the presence of low-cost airlines in more of those markets, lower air fares, fewer dominated markets, and a shrinking dominance by a single airline at some of the nation's largest airports. The average number of competitors in the largest 5,000 city-pair markets rose to 3.3 in 2006 from 2.9 in 1998. This growth is attributable to the increased presence of low-cost airlines, which increased nearly 60 percent. In addition, the number of largest 5,000 markets dominated by a single airline declined by 15 percent.

Airlines seek to merge with or acquire other airlines with the intention of increasing their profitability and financial sustainability, but must weigh these potential benefits against operational and regulatory costs and challenges. The principal benefits airlines consider are cost reductions—by combining complementary assets, eliminating duplicate activities, and reducing capacity—and increased revenues from higher fares in existing markets and increased demand for more seamless travel to more destinations. Balanced against these potential benefits are operational costs of integrating workforces, aircraft fleets, and systems. In addition, because most airline mergers and acquisitions are reviewed by DOJ, the relevant antitrust enforcement agency, airlines must consider the risks of DOJ opposition.

Both DOJ and DOT play a role in reviewing airline mergers and acquisitions, but DOJ's determination as to whether a proposed merger is likely substantially to lessen competition is key. DOJ uses an integrated analytical framework set forth in the *Horizontal Merger Guidelines* to make its determination. Under that process, DOJ assesses the extent of likely anticompetitive effects in the relevant markets, in this case, airline city-pair markets. DOJ further considers the likelihood that airlines entering these markets would counteract any anticompetitive effects. It also considers any efficiencies that a merger or acquisition could bring—for example, consumer benefits from an expanded route network. Our analysis of changes in the airline industry, such as increased competition and the growth of low-cost airlines, indicates that airline entry may be more likely now than in the past provided recent increases in fuel costs do not reverse these conditions. Additionally, the *Horizontal Merger Guidelines* have evolved to provide clarity as to the consideration of efficiencies, an important factor in airline mergers.

ABBREVIATIONS

ASM	available seat mile
BTC	Business Travel Coalition
CASM	cost per available seat mile
DOJ	Department of Justice
DOT	Department of Transportation
FAA	Federal Aviation Administration
GDP	gross domestic product
LCC	low-cost carrier
PBGC	Pension Benefit Guaranty Corporation
RPM	revenue per mile

July 31, 2008

The Honorable John D. Rockefeller, IV
Chairman
The Honorable Kay Bailey Hutchison
Ranking Member
Subcommittee on Aviation Operations, Safety, and Security
Committee on Commerce, Science, and Transportation
United States Senate

The passenger airline industry is vital to the U.S. economy, with operating revenues of nearly $172 billion in 2007, equivalent to over 1 percent of the U.S. gross domestic product. It also serves as an important engine for economic growth and a critical link in the nation's transportation infrastructure, carrying over 700 million passengers in 2007. The U.S. airline industry was deregulated in 1978, allowing market forces, rather than the federal government, to establish fares and service. Since 1978, the industry has experienced cyclical financial performance and numerous bankruptcies, mergers, and acquisitions, as the industry adjusted to an unregulated environment and changing market conditions.[1] In recent years, the financial condition of legacy, or network, airlines—the largest segment of the passenger airline industry—deteriorated significantly even by historical standards.[2] From 2001 to 2005, legacy airlines lost more than $33 billion, while four of them entered and exited bankruptcy. More recently, in 2006 and 2007 the airline industry returned to modest profitability only to confront rapidly increasing fuel costs and the expectation of renewed losses in 2008. These challenges and structural changes have spurred some airlines to explore mergers and acquisitions as a potential way to improve their competitive positions and financial viability—for example, Delta Air Lines and Northwest Airlines announced plans to merge on April 14, 2008.[3] Mergers and acquisitions, however, could also have anticompetitive effects, such as reduced competition and increased fares in some markets. Generally, before any airline merger or acquisition can be consummated, the Department of Justice (DOJ) carries out its antitrust enforcement responsibilities by evaluating whether the proposed merger is likely to substantially lessen competition and may challenge in court those that appear to be anticompetitive.

US Airways' attempt to acquire Delta Air Lines in 2006, the merger announcement between Delta Air Lines and Northwest Airlines earlier this year, and the continued focus on potential airline mergers and acquisitions prompted interest in a broad assessment of the state of the industry, the factors that are driving continued interest in mergers and acquisitions, and the process the federal government uses to assess them. In order to assist Congress in understanding possible future airline mergers and acquisitions, GAO was asked to describe (1) the financial condition of the U.S. passenger airline industry, (2) whether the industry is becoming more or less competitive, (3) why airlines seek to merge with or acquire other airlines, and (4) the role of federal authorities in considering airline mergers and acquisitions.

To address these objectives, we conducted analysis using Department of Transportation (DOT) financial and operating data, reviewed historical documents and past studies, and conducted interviews. Specifically, to evaluate the financial condition of the domestic airline industry, we analyzed airline financial metrics; reviewed financial studies; and conducted interviews with airline managers, trade associations, financial analysts, and other industry experts. Our financial analysis relied on airline financial data reported to DOT by airlines from 1998 through 2007, as these were the most recent and complete annual data available. To evaluate changes in airline industry competition, we analyzed data from DOT's Origin and Destination Survey, which includes fare and itinerary information on every 10th airline ticket sold; reviewed studies assessing competition; and interviewed current and former DOT officials and aviation industry experts. Our analysis of DOT data focused on passenger ticket data for the largest 5,000 domestic airline markets from 1998 through 2006.[4] We excluded tickets with international, Hawaiian, or Alaskan destinations or origins so that we could examine changes within contiguous domestic markets. To assess the reliability of all DOT data used by GAO, we reviewed the quality control procedures applied by DOT and subsequently determined that the data were sufficiently reliable for our purposes. To identify and evaluate the primary factors that airlines consider in deciding whether to merge with or acquire another airline, we reviewed studies and reports; assessed past airline mergers and acquisitions; and conducted interviews with DOT and DOJ officials, airline managers, financial analysts, academic researchers, and industry experts. In addition, to understand the government's role in evaluating a proposed merger or acquisition, we discussed the merger review processes with DOJ officials and antitrust experts and reviewed available documentation addressing past mergers and acquisitions. We conducted this performance audit from May 2007 through July 2008 in accordance with generally accepted government auditing standards. Those standards require that we plan and perform the audit to obtain sufficient, appropriate evidence to provide a reasonable basis for our findings and conclusions based on our audit objectives. We believe that the evidence obtained provides a reasonable basis for our findings and conclusions based on our audit objectives.

RESULTS IN BRIEF

The U.S. passenger airline industry was profitable in 2006 and 2007 for the first time since 2000, but high fuel prices will likely result in industry losses in 2008. Legacy airlines, which currently account for two-thirds of industry market share, realized collective operating profits of $1.8 billion in 2007, as compared to collective operating losses of nearly $33 billion from 2001 through 2005 which forced four legacy airlines into bankruptcy.[5] Legacy airlines generally improved their financial positions and returned to modest operating profitability in recent years by reducing operating costs and domestic capacity, while focusing on more profitable international markets. Low-cost airlines, meanwhile, have continued to maintain modest profitability since 1998. From 2003 through 2007, the airline industry experienced a relatively steady increase in passenger traffic—as measured by revenue passenger miles—growing 14 percent. At the same time, and unlike in past recoveries, industry capacity—as measured by available seat miles—increased 9 percent. Legacy airlines were also able to reduce costs, especially through bankruptcy, which triggered contract and pay concessions from labor unions and the termination and transfer of employee pension plans. Although the industry saw profits in 2007, according to first quarter 2008 financial results and updated industry forecasts for the rest of the year, the industry is expected to incur substantial losses in 2008. Rapidly increasing fuel prices are forcing airlines to cut capacity.

From 1998 through 2006, the U.S. domestic airline industry became more competitive, as reflected by an increase in the number of competitors serving city-pair markets[6] (e.g., New York–Los Angeles), the presence of low-cost airlines in more of those markets, lower average fares, fewer dominated markets, and a shrinking dominance by a single airline at some of the nation's largest airports. The largest 5,000 city-pair markets—which account for more than 90 percent of passenger traffic—were serviced by more competitors on average in 2006 than in 1998.[7] Overall, average fares have declined 20 percent in real terms since 1998, and the average number of competitors in the top 5,000 markets rose from 2.9 in 1998 to 3.3 in 2006.[8] During the same period, there was tremendous growth of low-cost airlines. The number of top 5,000 markets serviced by at least one low-cost airline increased nearly 60 percent, from approximately 1,300 markets in 1998 to over 2,000 markets in 2006. Further evidence of increased competition can be seen in the reduced number of dominated markets—where a single airline carries 50 percent or more of passengers—in the top 5,000 markets. The number of markets dominated decreased from about 3,500 in 1998 to about 3,000 in 2006. In addition, although legacy airlines continued to dominate many of the largest airports, carrying at least 50 percent of airport passenger traffic,[9] most saw a decrease in their share of total passenger traffic as more competitors—mainly low-cost airlines—moved in or expanded. In 2006, of the 30 largest airports, 16 were dominated by a single airline, but at 8 of those airports, the dominant airline had lost some passenger traffic since 1998.

Airlines consider mergers and acquisitions as a means to increase their profitability and financial viability, but must consider the operational and regulatory challenges to consummating a combination. Intended financial benefits stem from both cost reductions and increased revenues. Cost reductions may result from the elimination of duplicative operations—such as those at hubs or maintenance facilities—or by eliminating redundant city-pair service. On the revenue side, a merger or acquisition could generate additional revenues through increased fares on some routes as a result of capacity reductions or increased market share, although those fare increases may be transitory because other airlines could enter the affected markets and drive prices back down. Mergers or acquisitions could also attract more customers, and thus more revenue, by expanding airline networks to gain new city-pair combinations (domestically and internationally). Each merger or acquisition is different from others in terms of the extent to which cost reductions and revenue increases are factors. Balanced against these potential benefits are certain operational and regulatory challenges posed by mergers and acquisitions, which can be significant. For example, the integration of workforces is often particularly challenging and costly. New contracts must be negotiated, pilot seniority lists must be combined, and concessions may be required to gain labor support for mergers. Other significant operational challenges often involve the integration of aircraft fleets and information technology systems and processes. Demonstrating to DOJ, the relevant antitrust enforcement authority, that a merger or acquisition is not likely to be anticompetitive may also pose a significant challenge.

Both DOJ and DOT play a role in reviewing potential mergers and acquisitions, but DOJ's determination of whether a merger or acquisition is likely substantially to lessen competition is key. If DOJ believes the transaction is anticompetitive and would harm consumers, it may petition a court to prohibit the transaction. For airlines, and many other industries, DOJ uses an analytical framework set forth in the *Horizontal Merger Guidelines* (the Guidelines) to evaluate merger proposals.[10] As part of that framework, DOJ uses an integrated five-part process that assesses (1) the relevant market (city-pairs in the case of airlines); (2) the potential anticompetitive effects resulting from a merger or acquisition; (3) the likelihood and impact of other airlines possibly entering a market and counteracting any anticompetitive effects; (4) "efficiencies" (benefits) that a merger would bring—for example, consumer benefits from an expanded route network—and (5) whether one of the airlines proposing to merge would fail and its assets exit the market in the absence of a merger or acquisition. These considerations allow DOJ to determine whether it should challenge the merger because it would raise antitrust concerns. DOT also plays a role in the merger review process, providing competition data to DOJ, and if DOJ does not challenge the merger or acquisition, DOT may review the financial and safety standing of the new combined airline. Our analysis of changes in the airline industry, prior to the recent spike in fuel prices, indicates that the likelihood of airline entry increased. Additionally, the Guidelines have evolved to provide clarity as to the consideration of efficiencies, an important factor in airline mergers.

We provided a draft of this chapter to DOT and DOJ for their review and comment. Both DOT and DOJ officials provided some clarifying and technical comments that we incorporated where appropriate.

BACKGROUND

The U.S. airline industry is principally composed of legacy, low-cost, and regional airlines, and while it is largely free of economic regulation, it remains regulated in other respects, most notably safety, security, and operating standards. Legacy airlines—sometimes called network airlines—are essentially those airlines that were in operation before the Airline Deregulation Act of 1978 and whose goal is to provide service from "anywhere to everywhere."[11] To meet that goal, these airlines support large, complex hub-and-spoke operations with thousands of employees and hundreds of aircraft (of various types), with service at numerous fare levels to domestic communities of all sizes and to international destinations. To enhance revenues without expending capital, legacy airlines have entered into domestic (and international) alliances that give them access to some portion of each others' networks. Low-cost airlines generally entered the marketplace after deregulation and primarily operate less costly point-to-point service using fewer types of aircraft. Low-cost airlines typically offer simplified fare structures, which were originally aimed at leisure passengers but are increasingly attractive to business passengers because they typically do not have restrictive ticketing rules, which make it significantly more expensive to purchase tickets within 2 weeks of the flight or make changes to an existing itinerary. Regional airlines generally operate smaller aircraft—turboprops or regional jets with up to 100 seats—and provide service under code-sharing arrangements with larger legacy airlines on a cost-plus or fee-for-departure basis to smaller communities. Some regional airlines are owned by a legacy parent, while others are independent. For example, American Eagle is the regional partner for American Airlines, while independent Sky West Airlines operates on a fee-per-departure agreement with Delta Air Lines, United Airlines, and Midwest Airlines.[12]

The airline industry has experienced considerable merger and acquisition activity since its early years, especially immediately following deregulation in 1978 (Figure 1 provides a timeline of mergers and acquisitions for the eight largest surviving airlines). There was a flurry of mergers and acquisitions during the 1980s, when Delta Air Lines and Western Airlines merged, United Airlines acquired Pan Am's Pacific routes, Northwest acquired Republic Airlines, and American and Air California merged. In 1988, merger and acquisition review authority was transferred from DOT to DOJ. Since 1998, and despite tumultuous financial periods, fewer mergers and acquisitions have occurred. In 2001, American Airlines acquired the bankrupt airline TWA, and in 2005 America West acquired US Airways while the latter was in bankruptcy. Certain other attempts at merging during that time period failed because of opposition from DOJ or employees and creditors. For example, in 2000, an agreement was reached that allowed Northwest Airlines to acquire a 50 percent stake in Continental Airlines (with limited voting power) to resolve the antitrust suit brought by DOJ against Northwest's proposed acquisition of a controlling interest in Continental.[13] A proposed merger of United Airlines and US Airways in 2000 also resulted in opposition from DOJ, which found that, in its view, the merger would violate antitrust laws by reducing competition, increasing air fares, and harming consumers on airline routes throughout the United States. Although DOJ expressed its intent to sue to block the transaction, the parties abandoned the transaction before a suit was filed. More recently, the 2006 proposed merger of US Airways and Delta Air Lines fell apart because of opposition from Delta's pilots and some of its creditors, as well as its senior management.

Since the airline industry was deregulated in 1978, its earnings have been extremely volatile. In fact, despite considerable periods of strong growth and increased earnings, airlines have at times suffered such substantial financial distress that the industry has experienced recurrent bankruptcies and has failed to earn sufficient returns to cover capital costs in the long run. Many analysts view the industry as inherently unstable due to key demand and cost characteristics. In particular, demand for air travel is highly cyclical, not only in relation to the state of the economy, but also with respect to political, international, and even health-related events. Yet the cost characteristics of the industry appear to make it difficult for firms to rapidly contract in the face of declining demand. In particular, aircraft are expensive, long-lived capital assets. And as demand declines, airlines cannot easily reduce flight schedules in the very near term because passengers are already booked on flights for months in advance, nor can they quickly change their aircraft fleets. That is, airplane costs are largely fixed and unavoidable in the near term. Moreover, even though labor is generally viewed as a variable cost, airline employees are mostly unionized, and airlines find that they cannot reduce employment costs very quickly when demand for air travel slows. These cost characteristics can thus lead to considerable excess capacity in the face of declining demand. Finally, the industry is also susceptible to certain external shocks—such as those caused by fuel price volatility. In 2006 and 2007, the airline industry generally regained profitability after several very difficult years. However, these underlying fundamental characteristics of the industry suggest that it will remain an industry susceptible to rapid swings in its financial health.

Since deregulation in 1978, the financial stability of the airline industry has become a considerable concern for the federal government due to the level of financial assistance it has provided to the industry through assuming terminated pension plans and other forms of assistance. Since 1978 there have been over 160 airline bankruptcies. While most of these bankruptcies affected small airlines that were eventually liquidated, 4 of the more recent bankruptcies (Delta, Northwest, United, and US Airways) are among the largest corporate bankruptcies ever, excluding financial services firms. During these bankruptcies, United Airlines and US Airways terminated their pension plans and $9.7 billion in claims were shifted to the Pension Benefit Guarantee Corporation (PGBC).[14] Further, to respond to the shock to the industry from the September 11, 2001, terrorist attacks, the federal government provided airlines with $7.4 billion in direct assistance and authorized $1.6 billion (of $10 billion available) in loan guarantees to six airlines.[15]

Although the airline industry has experienced numerous mergers and bankruptcies since deregulation, growth of existing airlines and the entry of new airlines have contributed to a steady increase in capacity.[16] Previously, GAO reported that although one airline may reduce capacity or leave the market, capacity returns relatively quickly.[17] Likewise, while past mergers and acquisitions have, at least in part, sought to reduce capacity, any resulting declines in industry capacity have been short-lived, as existing airlines have expanded or new airlines have expanded. Capacity growth has slowed or declined just before and during recessions, but not as a result of large airline liquidations. Figure 2 shows capacity trends since 1979 and the dates of major mergers and acquisitions.

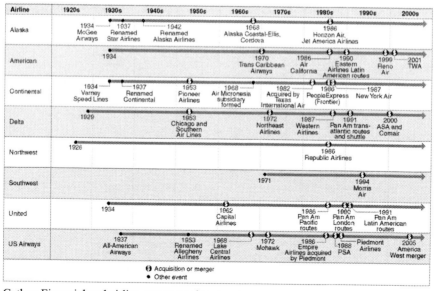

Sources: Cathay Financial and airline company documents.

Figure 1. Highlights of Domestic Airline Mergers and Acquisitions

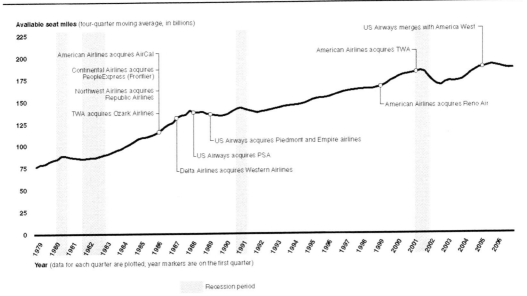

Sources: GAO analysis of Form 41 data, National Bureau of Economic Research, and DOT documents.

Figure 2. Growth of Industry Capacity and Major Airline Mergers and Acquisitions, 1979-2006

U.S. AIRLINES' FINANCIAL CONDITION HAS IMPROVED, BUT IT APPEARS TO BE SHORT-LIVED

The U.S. passenger airline industry has generally improved its financial condition in recent years, but its recovery appears short-lived because of rapidly increasing fuel prices. The U.S. airline industry recorded a net operating profit of $2.2 billion and $2.8 billion in 2006 and 2007, respectively,[18] the first time since 2000 that it had earned a profit. Legacy airlines—which lost nearly $33 billion between 2001 and 2005—returned to profitability in 2006 owing to increased passenger traffic, restrained capacity, and restructured costs. Meanwhile, low-cost airlines, which also saw increased passenger traffic, remained profitable overall by continuing to keep costs low, as compared to costs at the legacy airlines, and managing their growth. The airline industry's financial future remains uncertain and vulnerable to a number of internal and external events—particularly the rapidly increasing costs of fuel.

Both Legacy and Low-Cost Airlines Improved Their Financial Positions in 2006 and 2007

The airline industry achieved modest profitability in 2006 and continued that trend through 2007. The seven legacy airlines had operating profits of $1.1 billion in 2006 and $1.8 billion in 2007, after losses totaling nearly $33 billion from 2001 through 2005. The seven low-cost airlines, after reaching an operating profit low of nearly $55 million in 2004, also saw improvement, posting operating profits of almost $958 million in 2006 and $1 billion in 2007. Figure 3 shows U.S. airline operating profits since 1998.

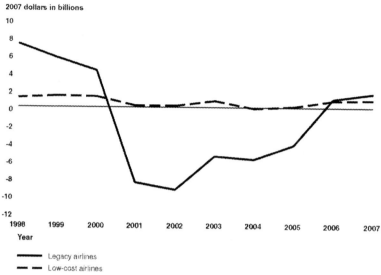

Source: GAO analysis of DOT data.

Note: Following their merger in 2005, US Airways and America West 2006-2007 data are included with the legacy airlines. America West's data from 1998 to 2005 are included with the low-cost airlines.

Figure 3. Operating Profit or Loss for Legacy and Low-Cost Airlines, 1998-2007

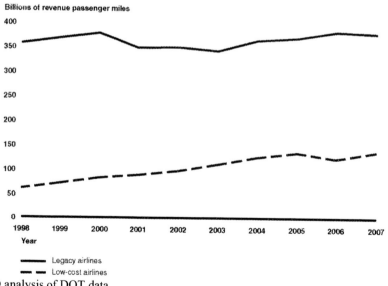

Source: GAO analysis of DOT data.

Note: Following their merger in 2005, US Airways and America West 2006-2007 data are included with the legacy airlines. America West's data from 1998 to 2005 are included with the low-cost airlines.

Figure 4. Revenue Passenger Miles among Legacy and Low-Cost Airlines, 1998-2007

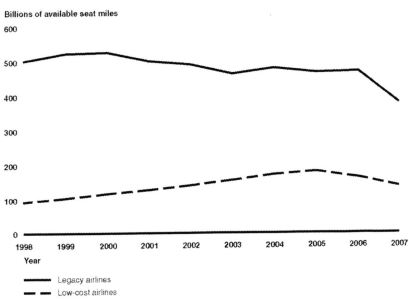

Source: GAO analysis of DOT data.

Note: Following their merger in 2005, US Airways and America West 2006-2007 data are included with the legacy airlines. America West's data from 1998 to 2005 are included with the low-cost airlines.

Figure 5. Domestic Available Seat Miles among Legacy and Low-Cost Airlines, 1998-2007

Increased Passenger Traffic and Capacity Restraint Have Improved Airline Revenues

An increase in passenger traffic since 2003 has helped improve airline revenues. Passenger traffic—as measured by revenue passenger miles (RPM)—increased for both legacy and low-cost airlines, as illustrated by figure 4.[19] Legacy airlines' RPMs rose 11 percent from 2003 through 2007, while low-cost airlines' RPMs grew 24 percent during the same period.

Airline revenues have also improved owing to domestic capacity restraint. Some past airline industry recoveries have been stalled because airlines grew their capacity too quickly in an effort to gain market share, and too much capacity undermined their ability to charge profitable fares. Total domestic capacity, as measured by available seat miles (ASM), increased 9 percent, from 696 billion ASMs in 2003 to 757 billion ASMs in 2007.[20] However, legacy airlines' ASMs declined 18 percent, from 460 billion in 2003 to 375 billion in 2007, as illustrated by figure 5. Industry experts and airline officials told us that legacy airlines reduced their domestic capacity, in part, by shifting capacity to their regional airline partners and to international routes. Even the faster growing low-cost airline segment saw a decline in ASMs in 2006 and 2007.

Since 2004, legacy airlines have shifted portions of their domestic capacity to more profitable international routes. From 1998 through 2003, the legacy airlines maintained virtually the same 30/70 percent capacity allocation split between international and domestic capacity. However, during the period from 2004 to 2007, legacy airlines increased their international capacity by 7 percentage points to a 37/63 percent split between international and domestic capacities. International expansion has proven to be a source of substantial new revenues for the legacy airlines because they often face less competition on international routes. Moreover, international routes generate additional passenger flow (and revenues) through their domestic networks, helping to support service over routes where competition from low-cost airlines has otherwise reduced legacy airlines' domestic revenues.

Cost Reduction and Bankruptcy Restructuring Efforts Have also Improved Airline Financial Positions

The airlines have also undertaken cost reduction efforts—much of which occurred through the bankruptcy process—in an attempt to improve their financial positions and better insulate themselves from the cyclical nature of the industry. Excluding fuel, unit operating costs for the industry, typically measured by cost per available seat mile,[21] have decreased 16 percent since reaching peak levels around 2001. A number of experts have pointed out that the legacy airlines have likely made most of the cost reductions that can be made without affecting safety or service; however, as figure 6 illustrates, a significant gap remains between legacy and low-cost airlines' unit costs. A recent expert study examining industry trends in competition and financial condition found similar results, also noting that the cost gap between legacy and low-cost airlines still exists.[22]

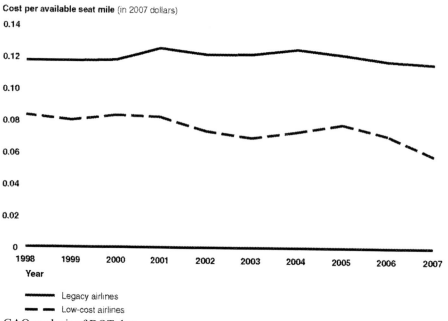

Source: GAO analysis of DOT data.

Note: Following their merger in 2005, US Airways and America West 2006-2007 data are included with the legacy airlines. America West's data from 1998 to 2005 are included with the low-cost airlines.

Figure 6. Unit Costs, Excluding Fuel, for Legacy and Low-Cost Airlines, 1998-2007

Many airlines achieved dramatic cuts in their operational costs by negotiating contract and pay concessions from their labor unions and through bankruptcy restructuring and personnel reductions. For example, Northwest Airlines pilots agreed to two pay cuts—15 percent in 2004 and an additional 23.9 percent in 2006, while in bankruptcy—to help the airline dramatically reduce operating expenses. Bankruptcy also allowed several airlines to significantly reduce their pension expenses, as some airlines terminated and shifted their pension obligations to PBGC. Legacy airlines in particular reduced personnel as another means of reducing costs. The average number of employees per legacy airline has decreased 26 percent, from 42,558 in 1998 to 31,346 in 2006. Low-cost airlines, on the other hand, have added personnel; however, they have done so in keeping with their increases in capacity. In fact, although total low-cost airline labor costs (including salaries and benefits) steadily increased from 1998 through 2007—from $2.8 billion to $5.0 billion—labor costs have accounted for roughly the same percentage (33 percent) of total operating expenses (including fuel) throughout the time period.

Although cost restructuring—achieved both through Chapter 11 bankruptcy reorganizations and outside of that process—has enabled most legacy airlines to improve their balance sheets in recent years, it still leaves the industry highly leveraged. Legacy airlines have significantly increased their total cash reserves from $2.7 billion in 1998 to $24 billion in 2007, thereby strengthening their cash and liquidity positions.[23] Low-cost airlines also increased their total cash reserves. Industry experts we spoke with stated that this buildup of cash reserves is a strategic move to help the airlines withstand future industry shocks, as well as to pay down debts or return value to stockholders. Experts, however, also agreed that debt is still a problem within the industry, particularly for the legacy airlines. For example, legacy airlines' assets-to-liabilities ratio (a measure of a firm's long-term solvency) is still less than 1 (assets less than liabilities). In 1998, legacy airlines' average ratio was 0.70, which improved only slightly to 0.74 in 2007. In contrast, while low-cost airlines have also added significant liabilities owing to their growth, their assets-to-liabilities ratio remains better than that of legacy airlines, increasing from 0.75 in 1998 to 1 in 2007.

Airlines' Financial Turnaround May Be Short-lived

Because the financial condition of the airline industry remains vulnerable to external shocks—such as the rising cost of fuel, economic downturns, or terrorist attacks—the near-term and longer-term financial health of the industry remains uncertain. In light of increased fuel prices and softening passenger demand, the profit and earnings outlook has reversed itself, and airlines may incur record losses in 2008. Although the industry saw profits in 2007 and some were predicting even larger profits in 2008, experts and industry analysts now estimate that the industry could incur significant losses in 2008. In fact, although estimates vary, one analyst recently projected $2.8 billion in industry losses, while another analyst put industrywide losses between $4 billion and $9 billion for the year, depending on demand trends. More recently, the airline trade association, the Air Transport Association, estimated losses of between $5 billion and $10 billion this year, primarily due to escalating fuel prices. For the first quarter of 2008, airlines reported net operating losses of more than $1.4 billion.

Fuel Costs Are Increasing and Other Costs May Increase

Many experts cite rising fuel costs as a key obstacle facing the airlines for the foreseeable future. The cost of jet fuel has become an ever-increasing challenge for airlines, as jet fuel climbed to over $2.85 per gallon in early 2008, and has continued to increase. By comparison, jet fuel was $1.11 per gallon in 2000, in 2008 dollars (Figure 7 illustrates the increase in jet fuel prices since 2000). Some airlines, particularly Southwest Airlines, reduced the impact of rising fuel prices on their costs through fuel hedges;[24] however, most of those airlines' hedges are limited or, in the case of Southwest, will expire within the next few years and may be replaced with new but more expensive hedges. In an attempt to curtail operating losses linked to higher fuel costs, most of the largest airlines have already announced plans to trim domestic capacity during 2008, and some have added baggage and other fees to their fares. Additionally, nine airlines have already filed for bankruptcy or ceased operations since December 2007, with many citing the significant increase in fuel costs as a contributing factor.[25]

In addition to rising fuel costs, other factors may strain airlines' financial health in the coming years. Labor contract issues are building at several of the legacy airlines, as labor groups seek to reverse some of the financial sacrifices that they made to help the airlines avoid or emerge from bankruptcy. Additionally, because bankruptcies required the airlines to reduce capital expenditures in order to bolster their balance sheets, needed investments in fleet renewal, new technologies, and product enhancements were delayed. Despite their generally sound financial condition as a group, some low-cost airlines may be facing cost increases as well. Airline analysts told us that some low-cost airline cost advantages may diminish as low-cost airlines begin to face cost pressures similar to those of the legacy airlines, including aging fleets—and their associated increased maintenance costs—and workforces with growing experience and seniority demanding higher pay.

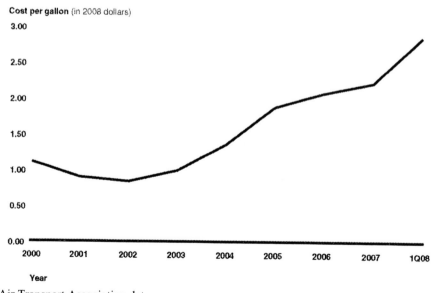

Source: Air Transport Association data.

Figure 7. Price of U.S. Jet Fuel, 2000—First Quarter 2008

Industry Faces Challenging Revenue Environment from Economic Downturns and Consumer Fare Expectations

The recent economic downturn and the long-term downward trend in fares create a challenging environment for revenue generation. Macroeconomic troubles—such as the recent tightening credit market and housing slump—have generally served as early indicators of reduced airline passenger demand. Currently, airlines are anticipating reduced demand by the fall of 2008. Additionally, domestic expansion of low-cost airline operations, as well as an increased ability of consumers to shop for lower fares more easily in recent years, has not only led to lower fares in general, but has also contributed to fare "compression"—that is, fewer very high-priced tickets are sold today than in the past. The downward pressure on ticket prices created by the increase of low-cost airline offerings is pervasive, according to a recent study and DOT testimony. Experts we spoke with explained that the increased penetration of low-fare airlines, combined with much greater transparency in fare pricing, has increased consumer resistance to higher fares.

DOMESTIC AIRLINE COMPETITION INCREASED FROM 1998 THROUGH 2006, AS LOW-COST AIRLINES EXPANDED

Competition within the U.S. domestic airline market increased from 1998 through 2006 as reflected by an increase in the average number of competitors in the top 5,000 city-pair markets,[26] the presence of low-cost airlines in more of these markets, lower fares, fewer dominated city-pair markets, and a shrinking dominance by a single airline at some of the nation's largest airports. The average number of competitors has increased in these markets from 2.9 in 1998 to 3.3 in 2006.[27] The number of these markets served by low-cost airlines increased by nearly 60 percent, from nearly 1,300 to approximately 2,000 from 1998 through 2006. Average round trip fares fell 20 percent, after adjusting for inflation, during the same period. Furthermore, approximately 500 fewer city-pair markets (15 percent) are dominated by a single airline. Similarly, competition has increased at the nation's 30 largest airports.

Average Number of Competitors and Low-Cost Airline Penetration Has Increased in the Top 5,000 Markets

The average number of competitors in the largest 5,000 city-pair market has increased since 1998. Overall, the average number of effective competitors—any airline that carries at least 5 percent of the traffic in that market—in the top 5,000 markets rose from 2.9 in 1998 to 3.3 in 2006. As figure 8 shows, the number of single airline (monopoly) markets decreased to less than 10 percent of the top 5,000 markets, while the number of markets with three or more airlines grew to almost 70 percent in 2006. Monopoly markets are generally the smallest city-pair markets, which lack enough traffic to support more than one airline.

Longer-distance markets are more competitive than shorter-distance markets. For example, among the top 5,000 markets in 2006, longer-distance markets (greater than 1,000 miles) had on average 3.9 competitors, while routes of less than 250 miles had on average only 1.7 competitors (Figure 9). The difference exists in large part because longer-distance markets have more viable options for connecting over more hubs.

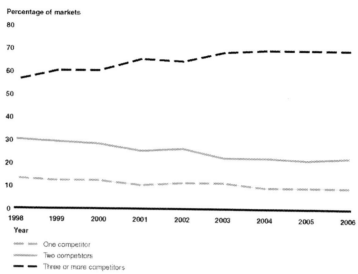

Source: GAO analysis of DOT data.

Note: This figure includes only passengers carried by an airline with at least 5 percent of the passengers in a city-pair market; therefore an unknown number of passengers in each market were not counted.

Figure 8. Markets by Number of Competitors, 1998-2006

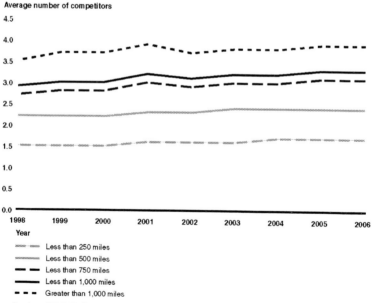

Source: GAO analysis of DOT data.

Note: This figure includes only passengers carried by an airline with at least 5 percent of passengers in a city-pair market; therefore an unknown number of passengers in each market were not counted.

Figure 9. Average Number of Competitors by Distance (in miles), Top 5,000 Markets, 1998-2006

For example, a passenger on a long-haul flight from Allentown, Pennsylvania, to Los Angeles, California—a distance of over 2,300 miles—would have options of connecting through 10 different hubs, including Cincinnati, Chicago, and Detroit. By comparison, a passenger from Seattle to Portland, Oregon—a distance of just under 300 miles—has no connection options, nor would connections be as attractive to passengers in short-haul markets.

Low-Cost Airlines Have Increased Their Presence among the Top 5,000 Markets

Low-cost airlines have increased the number of markets and passengers served and their overall market share since 1998. The number of the top 5,000 markets served by a low-cost airline jumped from approximately 1,300 to over 2,000 from 1998 through 2006, an increase of nearly 60 percent. Most of that increase is the result of low-cost airlines expanding their service into longer-haul markets than they typically served in 1998. Specifically, the number of markets served by low-cost airlines that were longer than 1,000 miles has increased by nearly 45 percent since 1998. For example, in 1998 Southwest Airlines served about 360 markets over 1,000 miles, and by 2006 it served over 670 such markets.

Low-cost airlines' expansion increased the extent to which they competed directly with legacy airlines. In 1998, low-cost airlines operated in 25 percent of the top 5,000 markets served by legacy airlines and provided a low-cost alternative to approximately 60 percent of passengers.[28] By 2006, low-cost airlines were competing directly with legacy airlines in 42 percent of the top 5,000 markets (an additional 756 markets) and provided a low-cost alternative to approximately 80 percent of passengers.

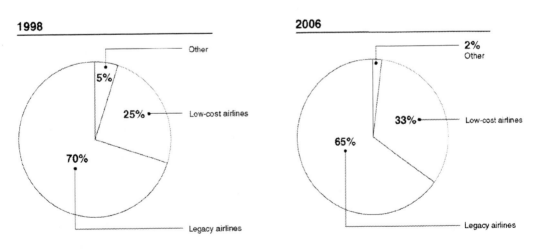

Note: These figures include only passengers carried by airlines with at least 5 percent of passengers in a city-pair market; therefore an unknown number of passengers in each market were not counted. The legacy airline category also includes regional airline passengers. The category "other" includes airlines not classified as legacy or low-cost airlines such as Hawaiian Airlines, Aloha Airlines, and Allegiant Air.

Figure 10. Industry Share by Legacy and Low-Cost Airlines, 1998 and 2006

In all, the growth of low-cost airlines into more markets and providing service to more passengers contributed to the shift in passenger traffic between legacy and low-cost airlines. Overall, low-cost airlines' share of passenger traffic increased from 25 percent in 1998 to 33 percent in 2006, while legacy airlines' domestic share of passenger traffic fell from 70 percent to 65 percent from 1998 through 2006 (see Figure 10). Low-cost airlines carried 78 million passengers in 1998 and 125 million in 2006—an increase of 59 percent.[29]

Average Fares Have Declined for Both Legacy and Low-Cost Airlines

Airfares in the top 5,000 markets, one of the key gauges of competition, have fallen in real terms since 1998. From 1998 through 2006, the round-trip average airfare fell from $198 to $161 (in 2006 dollars), a decrease of nearly 20 percent. As figure 11 shows, average fares have fallen across all distances. In 1998, average fares ranged from $257 for trips longer than 1,000 miles to $129 for trips of 250 miles or less. Since that time, however, fares have fallen considerably on the longest trips, and as of 2006, averaged just $183, a drop of 29 percent since 1998. Average fares for the shortest trips have not fallen as much. For trips of 250 miles or less, average fares as of 2006 have fallen 6 percent, to $121.

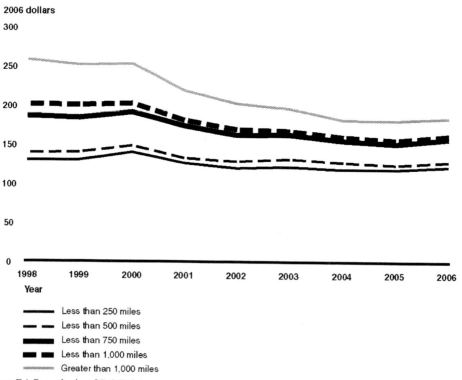

Source: GAO analysis of DOT data.

Note: This figure includes only passengers carried by an airline with at least 5 percent of passengers in a city-pair market, therefore an unknown number of passengers in each market were not counted.

Figure 11. Average Fares by Distance, 1998-2006

[Average fares tend to be lower in markets where low-cost airlines are present] Prior studies have shown that the presence of low-cost airlines in a market is associated with lower fares for all passengers in that market. In 1998, over 1,300 of the top 5,000 markets had a low-cost airline present, with an average fare of $167, as opposed to the 3,800 markets without low-cost competition, where the average fares averaged around $250. This same relationship was maintained in 2006, when low-cost airlines' presence grew to over 2,000 markets, and the average fare in these markets was $153, while the average fare in 2006 legacy airline-only markets was $194.[30]

Fewer Markets Are Dominated by a Single Airline

The number of the top 5,000 markets dominated by a single airline has declined. Since 1998, the number of dominated markets—markets with one airline with more than 50 percent of passengers—declined as competitors expanded into more markets. The number of dominated markets declined by approximately 500 markets, from 3,500 to 3,000 (or 15 percent) from 1998 through 2006, while the number of nondominated markets correspondingly rose by approximately 500, from approximately 1,400 to 1,900 markets (or 37 percent). (See Figure 12.)

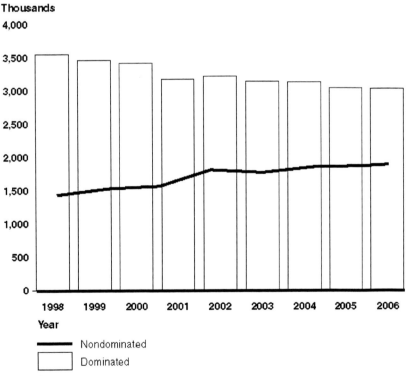

Source: GAO analysis of DOT data.
Note: This figure includes only passengers carried by an airline with at least 5 percent of passengers in a city-pair market; therefore an unknown number of passengers in each market were not counted.

Figure 12. The Number of Dominated and Nondominated Markets, Top 5,000 Markets, 1998-2006

Although there are fewer dominated markets among the top 5,000 markets, further analysis shows that low-cost airlines have increased their share of dominated markets while legacy airlines lost share. In 1998 legacy airlines dominated approximately 3,000 of the top 5,000 markets, but in 2006 that number fell to approximately 2,400. At the same time, low-cost airlines increased their share of dominated markets from about 300 markets in 1998 to approximately 500 markets. Appendix III shows the number of dominated markets by airline in 2006. Low-cost airlines tend to operate in larger dominated markets than legacy airlines. For example, in 2006, legacy airlines carried an average of 55,000 passengers per dominated market, while low-cost airlines carried an average of 165,000 passengers per dominated market.[31] This difference reflects the low-cost airlines' targeting of high-density markets and the nature of hub-and-spoke networks operated by legacy airlines.

Competition Has Increased at the Nation's Largest Airports

Competition has generally increased at the nation's largest airports. Airline dominance at many of the largest domestic airports in the United States has decreased as competition has increased in the industry. Although legacy airlines have a dominant position—carrying at least 50 percent of passenger traffic—at 16 of the nation's 30 largest airports.[32] One-half of these 16 dominated airports saw a decline in passenger traffic from 1998 through 2006 (see app. III). Of the 16 airports dominated by a single airline, 14 were dominated by legacy airlines. At 9 of these airports, the second largest airline carried less than 10 percent of passenger traffic, while at the other 5 airports a low-cost airline carried 10 percent or more of passenger traffic.

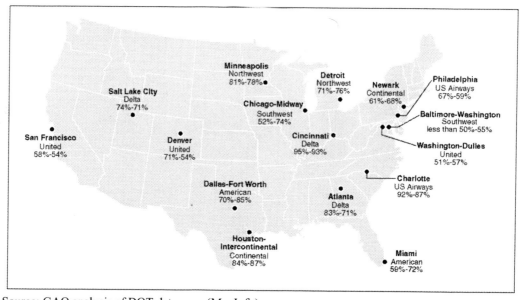

Source: GAO analysis of DOT data, map (MapInfo).

Figure 13. Change in Passenger Share at Selected Dominated Airports by Dominant Airline, 1998 and 2006

AIRLINES SEEK TO COMBINE TO INCREASE PROFITS AND IMPROVE FINANCIAL VIABILITY, BUT CHALLENGES EXIST

[Airlines seek mergers and acquisitions as a means to increase profitability and long-term financial viability, but must weigh those potential benefits against the operational and regulatory costs and challenges posed by combinations.]A merger's or acquisition's potential to increase short-term profitability and long-term financial viability stems from both anticipated cost reductions and increased revenues. Cost reductions may be achieved through merger-generated operating efficiencies—for example, through the elimination of duplicative operations. Cost savings may also flow from adjusting or reducing the combined airline's capacity and adjusting its mix of aircraft. Airlines may also seek mergers and acquisitions as a means to increase their revenues through increased fares in some markets—stemming from capacity reductions and increased market share in existing markets—and an expanded network, which creates more market pairs both domestically and internationally. Nonetheless, increased fares in these markets may be temporary because other airlines could enter the affected markets and drive fares back down. Mergers and acquisitions also present several potential challenges to airline partners, including labor and other integration issues—which may not only delay (or even preclude) consolidation, but also offset intended gains. DOJ antitrust review is another potential challenge, and one that we discuss in greater detail in the next section.

Airline Mergers and Acquisitions Aim to Increase Profitability by Reducing Costs and Increasing Revenues

[A merger or acquisition may produce cost savings by enabling an airline to reduce or eliminate duplicative operating costs.]Based on past mergers and acquisitions and experts we consulted, a range of potential cost reductions can result, such as the elimination of duplicative service, labor, and operations—including inefficient (or redundant) hubs or routes—and operational efficiencies from the integration of computer systems, and similar airline fleets.]Other cost savings may stem from facility consolidation, procurement savings, and working capital and balance sheet restructuring, such as renegotiating aircraft leases.] According to US Airways officials and analyst reports, for example, the merger of America West and US Airways generated $750 million in cost savings through the integration of information technology, combined overhead operations, and facilities closings.

Airlines may also pursue mergers or acquisitions to more efficiently manage capacity—both to reduce operating costs and to generate revenue—in their networks. A number of experts we spoke with stated that given recent economic pressures, particularly increased fuel costs, one motive for mergers and acquisitions is the opportunity to lower costs by reducing redundant capacity. Experts have said that industry mergers and acquisitions could lay the foundation for more rational capacity reductions in highly competitive domestic markets and could help mitigate the impact of economic cycles on airline cash flow. In addition, capacity reductions from a merger or acquisition could also serve to generate additional revenue through increased fares on some routes; over the long-term, however, those increased fares may be brought down because other airlines, especially low-cost airlines, could enter the affected markets and drive prices back down. In the absence of mergers and acquisitions and facing ongoing cost pressures, airlines have already begun to reduce their capacity in 2008.

Airlines may also seek to merge with or acquire an airline as a way to generate greater revenues from an expanded network, which serves more city-pair markets, better serves passengers, and thus enhances competition. Mergers and acquisitions may generate additional demand by providing consumers more domestic and international city-pair destinations. Airlines with expansive domestic and international networks and frequent flier benefits particularly appeal to business traffic, especially corporate accounts. Results from a recent Business Traveler Coalition (BTC) survey indicate that about 53 percent of the respondents were likely to choose a particular airline based upon the extent of its route network.[33] Therefore, airlines may use a merger or acquisition to enhance their networks and gain complementary routes, potentially giving the combined airline a stronger platform from which to compete in highly profitable markets.

Mergers and acquisitions can also be used to generate greater revenues through increased market share and fares on some routes. For example, some studies of airline mergers and acquisitions during the 1980s showed that prices were higher on some routes from the airline's hubs after the combination was completed.[34] At the same time, even if the combined airline is able to increase prices in some markets, the increase may be transitory if other airlines enter the markets with sufficient presence to counteract the price increase. In an empirical study of airline mergers and acquisitions up to 1992, Winston and Morrison suggest that being able to raise prices or stifle competition does not play a large role in airlines' merger and acquisition decisions.[35] Numerous studies have shown, though, that increased airline dominance at an airport results in increased fare premiums, in part because of competitive barriers to entry.[36] Several recent merger and acquisition attempts (United and US Airways in 2000, Northwest and Continental in 1998) were blocked because of opposition by DOJ because of concerns about anticompetitive impacts. Ultimately, however, each merger and acquisition differs in the extent to which cost reductions and revenue increases are factors.

Cost reductions and the opportunity to obtain increased revenue could serve to bolster a merged airline's financial condition, enabling the airline to better compete in a highly competitive international environment. For example, officials from US Airways stated that as a result of its merger with America West, the airline achieved a significant financial transformation, and they cited this as a reason why airlines merge. Many industry experts believe that the United States will need larger, more economically stable airlines to be able to compete with the merging and larger foreign airlines that are emerging in the global economy. The airline industry is becoming increasingly global; for example, the Open Skies agreement between the United States and the European Union became effective in March 2008.[37] Open Skies has eliminated previous government controls on these routes (especially to and from London's Heathrow Airport), presenting U.S. and European Union airlines with great opportunities as well as competition. In order to become better prepared to compete under Open Skies, global team antitrust immunity applications have already been filed with DOT.[38] Antitrust immune alliances differ from current code-share agreements or alliance group partnerships because they allow partners not only to code-share but also to jointly plan and market their routes and schedules, share revenue, and possibly even jointly operate flights.[39] According to one industry analyst, this close global cooperation may facilitate domestic consolidation as global alliance partners focus on maximizing synergies for both increasing revenues and reducing costs with their global alliance teams.

Potential Challenges to Mergers and Acquisitions Include Integration Issues and Regulatory Challenges

We identified a number of potential barriers to consummating a combination, especially in terms of operational challenges that could offset a merger's or acquisition's intended gains. The most significant operational challenges involve the integration of workforces, organizational cultures, aircraft fleets, and information technology systems and processes. Indeed, past airline mergers and acquisitions have proven to be difficult, disruptive, and expensive, with costs in some cases increasing in the short term as the airlines integrate. Airlines also face potential challenges to mergers and acquisitions from DOJ's antitrust review, discussed in the next section.

Workforce integration is often particularly challenging and expensive, and involves negotiation of new labor contracts. Labor groups—including pilots, flight attendants, and mechanics—may be able to demand concessions from the merging airlines during these negotiations, several experts explained, because labor support would likely be required in order for a merger or acquisition to be successful. Some experts also note that labor has typically failed to support mergers, fearing employment or salary reductions. Obtaining agreement from each airline's pilots' union on an integrated pilot seniority list—which determines pilots' salaries, as well as what equipment they can fly—may be particularly difficult. According to some experts, as a result of these labor integration issues and the challenges of merging two work cultures, airline mergers have generally been unsuccessful. For example, although the 2005 America West–US Airways merger has been termed a successful merger by many industry observers, labor disagreements regarding employee seniority, and especially pilot seniority, remain unresolved. More recently, labor integration issues derailed merger talks—albeit temporarily—between Northwest Airlines and Delta Air Lines in early 2008, when the airlines' labor unions were unable to agree on pilot seniority list integration. Recently, the Consolidated Appropriations Act of 2008 included a labor protective provision that applies to the integration of employees of covered air carriers, and could affect this issue.[40] Furthermore, the existence of distinct corporate cultures can influence whether two firms will be able to merge their operations successfully. For example, merger discussions between United Airlines and US Airways broke down in 1995 because the employee-owners of United feared that the airlines' corporate cultures would clash.

The integration of two disparate aircraft fleets may also be costly. Combining two fleets may increase costs associated with pilot training, maintenance, and spare parts. For example, a merger between Northwest and Delta would result in an airline with 10 different aircraft types. These costs may, however, be reduced post-merger by phasing out certain aircraft from the fleet mix. Pioneered by Southwest and copied by other low-cost airlines, simplified fleets have enabled airlines to lower costs by streamlining maintenance operations and reducing training times. If an airline can establish a simplified fleet, or "fleet commonality"—particularly by achieving an efficient scale in a particular aircraft—then many of the cost efficiencies of a merger or acquisition may be set in motion by facilitating pilot training, crew scheduling, maintenance integration, and inventory rationalization.

Finally, integrating information technology processes and systems can also be problematic and time-consuming for a merging airline. For example, officials at US Airways told us that while some cost reductions were achieved within 3 to 6 months of its merger with America West, the integration of information technology processes has taken nearly 2 ½ years. Systems integration issues are increasingly daunting as airlines attempt to integrate a complex mix of modern in-house systems, dated mainframe systems, and outsourced information technology. The US Airways-America West merger highlighted the potential challenges associated with combining reservations systems, as there were initial integration problems.

THE DEPARTMENT OF JUSTICE'S ANTITRUST REVIEW IS A CRITICAL STEP IN THE AIRLINE MERGER AND ACQUISITION PROCESS

The DOJ's review of airline mergers and acquisitions is a key step for airlines hoping to consummate a merger. The Guidelines provide a five-part integrated process under which mergers and acquisitions are assessed by DOJ. In addition, DOT plays an advisory role for DOJ and, if the combination is consummated, may conduct financial and safety reviews of the combined entity under its regulatory authority. Public statements by DOJ officials and a review of the few airline mergers and acquisitions evaluated by DOJ over the last 10 years also provide some insight into how DOJ applies the Guidelines to the airline industry. While each merger and acquisition review is case specific, our analysis shows that changes in the airline industry, such as increased competition in international and domestic markets, could lead to entry being more likely than in the past. Additionally, the Guidelines have evolved to provide clarity as to the consideration of efficiencies, an important factor in airline mergers.

The Department of Justice Uses the Guidelines to Identify Antitrust Concerns

Most proposed mergers or acquisitions must be reviewed by DOJ. In particular, under the Hart-Scott-Rodino Act, an acquisition of voting securities and/or assets above a set monetary amount must be reported to DOJ (or the Federal Trade Commission for certain industries) so the department can determine whether the merger or acquisition poses any antitrust concerns.[41] To analyze whether a proposed merger or acquisition raises antitrust concerns— whether the proposal will create or enhance market power or facilitate its exercise[42]—DOJ follows an integrated five-part analytical process set forth in the Guidelines.[43] First, DOJ defines the relevant product and geographic markets in which the companies operate and determines whether the merger is likely to significantly increase concentration in those markets. Second, DOJ examines potential adverse competitive effects of the merger, such as whether the merged airlines will be able to charge higher prices or restrict output for the product or service it sells. Third, DOJ considers whether other competitors are likely to enter the affected markets and whether they would counteract any potential anticompetitive effects that the merger might have posed. Fourth, DOJ examines the verified "merger specific" efficiencies or other competitive benefits that may be generated by the merger and that cannot be obtained through any other practical means. Fifth, DOJ considers whether, absent the merger or acquisition, one of the firms is likely to fail, causing its assets to exit the market. The commentary to the Guidelines makes clear that DOJ does not apply the Guidelines as a step-by-step progression, but rather as an integrated approach in deciding whether the proposed merger or acquisition would create antitrust concerns.

DOJ first assesses competitive effects at a city-pair market level. In its review of past airline mergers and acquisitions, DOJ defined the relevant market as scheduled airline service between individual city-pair markets because, according to DOJ, that is the where airlines compete for passengers.[44] Second, DOJ assesses likely potential adverse competitive effects--specifically, whether a merged airline is likely to exert market power (maintain prices above competitive levels for a significant period of time) in particular city-pair markets. Generally, a merger or acquisition raises anticompetitive concerns to the extent it eliminates a competitor from the markets that both airlines competed in.[45] When United Airlines and US Airways proposed merging in 2000, DOJ concluded that the proposed merger would create monopolies or duopolies in 30 markets with $1.6 billion in revenues, lead to higher fares, and harm consumers on airline routes throughout the United States and on some international routes. The department was particularly concerned about reduced competition in certain markets—nonstop city-pair markets comprising the two airlines' hub airports, certain other nonstop markets on the East Coast that were served by both airlines, some markets served via connecting service by these airlines along the East Coast, and certain other markets previously dominated by one or both of these airlines. DOJ estimated that the merger would have resulted in higher air fares for businesses and millions of customers. Similarly, in 2000 DOJ sought divestiture by Northwest Airlines of shares in Continental Airlines after the airline had acquired more than 50 percent of the voting interest in Continental. DOJ argued that the acquisition would particularly harm consumers in 7 city-pair markets that linked Northwest and Continental airport hubs, where the two airlines had a virtual duopoly. DOJ also pointed to potential systemwide effects of removing a large competitor. Although DOJ objected to the proposed merger of United and US Airways and the acquisition of Continental by Northwest, it did not challenge a merger between America West and US Airways in 2005 because it found little overlap between city-pair markets served by the two airlines.

DOJ, under the Guidelines' third element, assesses whether new entry would counter the increased market power of a merged airline. If DOJ determines that the merger is likely to give the merging airlines the ability to raise prices or curtail service in a city-pair market, DOJ assesses whether a new entrant would likely begin serving the city-pair in response to a potential price increase to replace the lost competition and deter or counter the price increase. For such entry to resolve concerns about a market, the Guidelines require that it be "timely, likely, and sufficient" to counteract the likely anticompetitive effects presented by the merger. According to DOJ, the inquiry considers an entry time horizon of 2 years and is fact specific rather than based on theory.[46] Some factors that may be considered in assessing likelihood of entry include whether a potential entrant has a hub in one of the cities in a city-pair market of concern so that the potential entrant is well placed to begin service, whether there are constraints (such as slot controls or shortage of gates) that could limit effective entry, and whether the potential entrant would be able to provide the frequency of service that would be required to counteract the merged firm's presence. For example, if the merging parties operate the only hubs at both end points of a market, it is unlikely that a new entrant airline would find it profitable to offer an effective level of service. In its complaint challenging Northwest Airlines' attempted acquisition of a controlling interest in Continental, DOJ alleged that significant entry barriers limited new competition for the specific city-pair markets of issue. For example, the complaint alleged that airlines without a hub at one of the end points of the affected hub-to-hub markets were unlikely to enter due to the cost advantages of the incumbents serving that market. In city-pair markets where the merging airlines would have a large share of passengers traveling on connecting flights, DOJ asserted that other airlines were unlikely to enter due to factors such as the light traffic on these routes and the proximity of Northwest's and Continental's hubs to the markets as compared to other airlines' more distant hubs.

Fourth, DOJ considers whether merger-specific efficiencies are "cognizable," that is, whether they can be verified and do not arise from anticompetitive reductions in output or services. Cognizable efficiencies, while not specifically defined under the Guidelines, could include any consumer benefit resulting from a merger—including enhanced service through an expanded route network and more seamless travel—as well as cost savings accruing to the merged airline (for example, from reducing overhead or increased purchasing power that may ultimately benefit the consumer).[47] Because efficiencies are difficult to quantify and verify, DOJ requires merger partners to substantiate merger benefits. DOJ considers only those efficiencies likely to be accomplished by the proposed merger and unlikely to be achieved through practical, less restrictive alternatives, such as code-sharing agreements or alliances. For example, in its October 2000 complaint against Northwest Airlines for its acquisition of a controlling interest in Continental, DOJ noted that Northwest had not adequately demonstrated that the efficiencies it claimed from the merger could not be gained from other, less anticompetitive means, particularly their marketing alliance, which DOJ did not challenge.

Finally, DOJ considers the financial standing of merger partners—if one of the partners is likely to fail without the merger and its assets were to exit the market. According to the Guidelines, a merger isn't likely to create or enhance market power or facilitate its exercise if imminent failure of one of the merging firms would cause the assets of that firm to exit the relevant market. For instance, the acquisition of TWA by American Airlines in 2001 was cleared because TWA was not likely to emerge from its third bankruptcy and there was no less anticompetitive purchaser.

In making its decision as to whether the proposed merger is likely anticompetitive— whether it is likely to create or enhance market power or facilitate its exercise—DOJ considers the particular circumstances of the merger as it relates to the Guidelines' five-part inquiry. The greater the potential anticompetitive effects, the greater must be the offsetting verifiable efficiencies for DOJ to clear a merger. However, according to the Guidelines, efficiencies almost never justify a merger if it would create a monopoly or near monopoly. If DOJ concludes that a merger threatens to deprive consumers of the benefits of competitive air service, then it will seek injunctive relief in a court proceeding to block the merger from being consummated. In some cases, the parties may agree to modify the proposal to address anticompetitive concerns identified by DOJ—for example, selling airport assets or giving up slots at congested airports—in which case DOJ ordinarily files a complaint along with a consent decree that embodies the agreed-upon changes.

The Department of Transportation also Reviews Proposed Mergers to Ensure That They Are in the Public Interest

DOT conducts its own analyses of airline mergers and acquisitions. While DOJ is responsible for upholding antitrust laws, DOT will conduct its own competitive analysis and provide it to DOJ in an advisory capacity. In addition, presuming the merger moves forward after DOJ review, DOT can undertake several other reviews if the situation warrants it. Before commencing operations, any new, acquired, or merged airlines must obtain separate authorizations from DOT—"economic" authority from the Office of the Secretary and "safety" authority from the Federal Aviation Administration (FAA). The Office of the Secretary is responsible for deciding whether applicants are fit, willing, and able to perform the service or provide transportation. To make this decision, the Secretary assesses whether the applicants have the managerial competence, disposition to comply with regulations, and financial resources necessary to operate a new airline. FAA is responsible for certifying that the aircraft and operations conform to the safety standards prescribed by the Administrator, for instance, that the applicants' manuals, aircraft, facilities, and personnel meet federal safety standards. Also, if a merger or other corporate transaction involves the transfer of international route authority, DOT is responsible for assessing and approving all transfers to ensure that they are consistent with the public interest. DOT is responsible for approving such matters to ensure that they are consistent with the public interest.[48] Finally, DOT also reviews the merits of any airline merger or acquisition and submits its views and relevant information in its possession to the DOJ. DOT also provides some essential data that DOJ uses in its review.

Changes in the Airline Industry and in the Guidelines May Affect the Factors Considered in DOJ's Merger Review Process

Changes in the airline industry's structure and in the Guidelines may affect the factors considered in DOJ's merger review process. DOJ's review is not static, as it considers both market conditions and current antitrust thinking at the time of the merger review. According to our own analysis and other studies, the industry has grown more competitive in recent years, and if that trend is not reversed by increased fuel prices, it will become more likely that market entry by other airlines, and possibly low-cost airlines, will bring fares back down in markets in which competition is initially reduced due to a merger. In addition, the ongoing liberalization of international markets and, in particular, cross-Atlantic routes under the U.S.-European Union Open Skies agreement, has led to increased competition on these routes. Finally, as DOJ and the Federal Trade Commission have evolved in their understanding of how to integrate merger-specific efficiencies into the evaluation process, the Guidelines have also changed.

Increased Competition Indicates That Airline Entry May Be More Likely than in the Past

A variety of characteristics of the current airline marketplace indicate that airline entry into markets vacated by a merger partner may be more likely than in the past, unless higher fuel prices substantially alter recent competitive trends in the industry. First, as we have noted, competition on airline routes—spurred by the growth and penetration of low-cost airlines—has increased, while the dominance of legacy airlines has been mitigated in recent years. According to our study, about 80 percent of passengers are now flying routes on which at least one low-cost airline is present. Moreover, some academic studies suggest that low-cost carrier presence has become a key factor in competition and pricing in the industry in recent years. Two articles suggest that the presence of Southwest Airlines on routes leads to lower fares and that even their presence—or entry into end-point airports of a market pair—may be associated with lower prices on routes.[49] Another recent study found that fare differentials between hub and nonhub airports—once measured to be quite substantial—are not as great as they used to be, which suggests a declining relevance of market power stemming from airline hub dominance.[50] The study did find, however that when there is little presence of low-cost airlines at a major carrier's hub airport, the hub premium continues to remain substantial. However, our competition analysis and these studies predate the considerable increase in fuel prices that has occurred this year and, if permanent, could affect competition and airlines' willingness to expand into new markets.

In some past cases, DOJ rejected the contention that new entry will be timely, likely, and sufficient to counter potential anticompetitive effects. For example, in 2000, when DOJ challenged Northwest Airline's proposed acquisition of a controlling interest in Continental Airlines, a DOJ official explained that the department considered it unrealistic to assume that the prospect of potential competition—meaning the possibility of entry into affected markets by other airlines—would fully address anticompetitive concerns, given network airline hub economics at the time.[51]

Merger Guidelines Have Evolved to Reflect Federal Antitrust Authorities' Greater Understanding of Efficiencies

The Guidelines have been revised several times over the years, and particularly the most recent revision, in 1997, reflects a greater understanding by federal antitrust authorities in how to assess and weigh efficiencies. In 1968, the consideration of efficiencies was allowed only as a defense in exceptional circumstances. In 1984, the Guidelines were revised to incorporate efficiencies as part of the competitive effects analysis, rather than as a defense. However, the 1984 Guidelines also required "clear and convincing" evidence that a merger will achieve significant net efficiencies. In 1992, the Guidelines were revised again, eliminating the "clear and convincing" standard. The 1997 revision explains that efficiencies must be "cognizable," that is, merger-specific efficiencies that can be verified and are net of any costs and not resulting solely from a reduction in service or output. In considering the efficiencies, DOJ weighs whether the efficiencies may offset the anticompetitive effects in each market.[52] According to the Guidelines, in some cases, merger efficiencies are not strictly in the relevant market, but are so inextricably linked with it that a partial divestiture or other remedy could not feasibly eliminate the anticompetitive effect in the relevant market without sacrificing the efficiencies in other markets.[53] Under those circumstances, DOJ will take into account across-the-board efficiencies or efficiencies that are realized in markets other than those in which the harm occurs. According to DOJ and outside experts, the evolution of the Guidelines reflects an attempt to provide clarity as to the consideration of efficiencies, an important factor in the merger review process.

APPENDIX I. SCOPE AND METHODOLOGY

To review the financial condition of the U.S. airline industry, we analyzed financial and operational data, reviewed relevant studies, and interviewed industry experts. We analyzed DOT Form 41 financial and operational data submitted to DOT by airlines between the years 1998 through 2007. We obtained these data from BACK Aviation Solutions, a private contractor that provides online access to U.S. airline financial, operational, and passenger data with a query-based user interface. To assess the reliability of these data, we reviewed the quality control procedures used by BACK Aviation and DOT and subsequently determined that the data were sufficiently reliable for our purposes. We also reviewed government and expert data analyses, research, and studies, as well as our own previous studies. The expert research and studies, where applicable, were reviewed by a GAO economist or were corroborated with additional sources to determine that they were sufficiently reliable for our purposes. Finally, we conducted interviews with government officials, airlines and their trade associations, credit and equity analysts, industry experts, and academics. The analysts, experts, and academics were identified and selected based on literature review, prior GAO work, and recommendations from within the industry.

To determine if and how the competitiveness of the U.S. airline industry has changed since 1998, we obtained and stratified DOT quarterly data on the 5,000 largest city-pair markets for calendar years 1998 through 2006. These data are collected by DOT based on a 10 percent random sampling of tickets and identify the origin and destination airports. These markets accounted for about 90 percent of all passengers in 2006. We excluded tickets with interlined flights—a flight in which a passenger transfers from one to another unaffiliated airline—and tickets with international, Alaskan, or Hawaiian destinations. Since only the airline issuing the ticket is identified, regional airline traffic is counted under the legacy parent or partner airline. To assess the reliability of these data, we reviewed the quality control procedures DOT applies and subsequently determined that the data were sufficiently reliable for our purposes. To analyze changes in competition based on the size of the passenger markets, we divided the markets into four groupings. Each group is composed of one-quarter of the total passenger traffic in each year. To stratify these markets by the number of effective competitors operating in a market, we used the following categories: one, two, three, four, and five or more effective competitors, where a airline needed to have at least a 5 percent share of the passengers in the city-pair market to be considered an effective competitor in that market. To stratify the data by market distance, we obtained the great circle distance for each market using the DOT ticket data via BACK Aviation and then grouped the markets into five distance categories: up to 250 miles, 251-500 miles, 501-750 miles, 751-

1,000 miles, and 1,001 miles and over. For the purposes of this study, we divided the airline industry into legacy and low-cost airlines. While there is variation in the size and financial condition of the airlines in each of these groups, there are more similarities than differences for airlines in each group. Each of the legacy airlines predate the airline deregulation of 1978, and all have adopted a hub-and-spoke network model, can be more expensive to operate than a simple point-to-point service model. Low-cost airlines have generally entered interstate competition since 1978,[54] are smaller, and generally employ a less costly point-to-point service model. Furthermore, the seven low-cost airlines (Air Tran, America West, ATA, Frontier, JetBlue, Southwest, and Spirit)[55] had consistently lower unit costs than the seven legacy airlines (Alaska, American, Continental, Delta, Northwest, United, and US Airways). For this analysis, we continued to categorize US Airways as a legacy airline following its merger with America West in 2005, and included the data for both airlines for 2006 and 2007 with the legacy airlines and between 1998 through 2005 we categorized America West as a low-cost airline.

To determine if competition has changed at the 30 largest airports, we analyzed DOT T-100 enplanement data for 1998 and 2006 to examine the changes in passenger traffic among the airlines at each airport. The T-100 database includes traffic data (passenger and cargo), capacity data, and other operational data for U.S. airlines and foreign airlines operating to and from the United States. The T-100 and T-100(f) data files are not based on sampled data or data surveys, but represent a 100 percent census of the data. To assess the reliability of these data, we reviewed the quality control procedures DOT applies and subsequently determined that the data were sufficiently reliable for our purposes.

To determine the potential effects on competition between the merger of Delta Air Lines and Northwest Airlines explained in appendix II, we examined whether the merger might reduce competition within given airline markets. We defined an effective competitor as an airline that has a market share of at least 5 percent. To examine the potential loss of competition under the merger, we determined the extent to which each airline's routes overlap by analyzing 2006 data from DOT on the 5,000 busiest domestic city-pair origin and destination markets. To determine the potential loss of competition in small communities, we analyzed origin and destination data (OD1B) for the third quarter of 2007 to determine the extent to which airlines' routes overlap. We defined small communities as those communities with airports that are defined as "nonhubs" by statute in 49 U.S.C. § 47102(13).[56]

To identify the key factors that airlines consider in deciding whether to merge with or acquire another airline, we reviewed relevant studies and interviewed industry experts. We reviewed relevant studies and documentation on past and prospective airline mergers in order to identify the factors contributing to (or inhibiting) those transactions. We also met with DOT and Department of Justice (DOJ) officials, airline executives, financial analysts, academic researchers, and industry consultants to discuss these factors and their relative importance.

To understand the process and approach used by federal authorities in considering airline mergers and acquisitions, we reviewed past and present versions of the Guidelines, DOT statutes and regulations, and other relevant guidance. We also analyzed legal documents from past airline mergers and published statements by DOT and DOJ officials to provide additional insight into how DOJ and DOT evaluate merger transactions. Finally, we discussed the merger review process with DOJ and DOT officials and legal experts. We conducted this performance audit from May 2007 through July 2008 in accordance with generally accepted government auditing standards. Those standards require that we plan and perform the audit to obtain sufficient, appropriate evidence to provide a reasonable basis for our findings and conclusions based on our audit objectives. We believe that the evidence obtained provides a reasonable basis for our findings and conclusions based on our audit objectives.

APPENDIX II. DELTA AND NORTHWEST MERGER

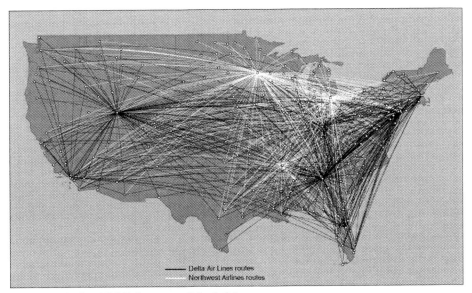

Source: GAO analysis of OAG data, map (MapInfo).
Note: Route map excludes Alaska and Hawaii routes.

Figure 14. Delta Air Lines and Northwest Airlines Domestic (lower 48) Route Map, February 2008 based on Official Airline Guide (OAG) Schedule Data

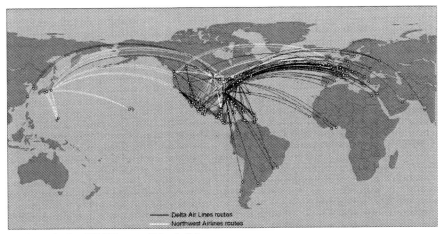

Source: GAO analysis of DOT, map (MapInfo).

Figure 15. Delta Air Lines and Northwest Airlines International Route Map, February 2008 based on OAG Schedule Data

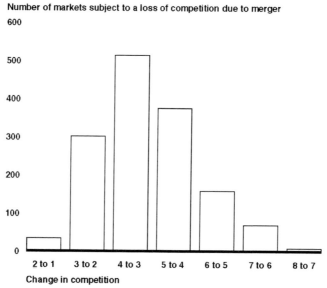

Source: GAO analysis of DOT data.

Figure 16. Number of Nonstop and One-Stop Markets Where Delta and Northwest Compete, Top 5,000 Markets, 2006

Table 1. Top Five Markets Where Competition Could Be Reduced from Two Airlines to One Airline, 2006

Market (city-pair)	Passengers	Percentage of total
Cincinnati, OH–Minneapolis, MN	54,240	13.5%
Fort Walton Beach, FL–Washington, DC	31,050	7.8%
Cincinnati, OH–Detroit. MI	28,870	7.2%
Cincinnati, OH–Manchester, NH	23,070	5.8%
Panama City, FL–Washington, DC	17,480	4.3%
Subtotal top five	154,710	38%
Remaining 29 markets	247,230	62%

analysis of DOT data.

Note: Passengers are included only if carried by an airline that was considered an effective competitor with at least 5 percent of the passengers in a city-pair market; therefore an unidentifiable number of passengers in each is not represented.

Table 2. Top Five Markets Where Competition Could Be Reduced from Three Airlines to Two Airlines, 2006

Market (city-pair)	Combined Market share	Second largest competitor	Second largest competitor Market share
Atlanta, GA–Detroit, MI	78%	AirTran	20%
Atlanta, GA–Minneapolis, MN	79%	AirTran	18%

Table 2. (Continued)

Market (city-pair)	Combined Market share	Second largest competitor	Second largest competitor Market share
Atlanta, GA–Memphis, TN	67%	AirTran	33%
Memphis, TN-Orlando, FL	80%	AirTran	12%
Memphis, TN–Tampa, FL	82%	AirTran	10%

Source: GAO analysis of DOT data.

Note: Passengers are included only if carried by an airline that was considered an effective competitor with at least 5 percent of the passengers in a city-pair market; therefore an unidentifiable number of passengers in each is not represented.

Table 3. Small Communities (Nonhub Airports) Where Delta and Northwest Have Service and Where Competition Could Be Reduced as of Third Quarter 2007

Change in competition			
2 to 1	3 to 2	4 to 3	5 to 4
Panama City, FL Tupelo, MS	Alexandria, LA Appleton, WI Bloomington, IL Casper, WY Charlottesville, VA Erie, PA Evansville, IN Fort Smith, AR Lafayette, LA Tri City, TN	Asheville, NC Binghamton, NY Bozeman, MT Charleston, WV Jackson, WY Kalamazoo, MI Monroe, LA Montgomery, AL Peoria, IL Rapid City, SD Roanoke, VA Sioux Falls, SD Traverse City, MI	Great Falls, MT Missoula, MT

Source: GAO analysis of DOT data.

Note: Passengers are included only if carried by an airline that was considered an effective competitor with at least 5 percent of the passengers in a city-pair market; therefore an unidentifiable number of passengers in each are not represented.

APPENDIX III. NUMBER AND SIZE OF DOMINATED MARKETS BY AIRLINE IN THE TOP 5,000 MARKETS, 2006

	Number of markets	Passengers
Southwest	407	55,065,710
Delta	643	21,433,770
American	325	18,297,130
Northwest	464	15,530,460
Continental	201	11,211,870
US Airways	444	11,133,960

Table. (Continued)

	Number of markets	Passengers
United	266	8,820,110
Alaska	92	7,248,730
AirTran	60	2,991,470
Midwest	29	2,314,120
Allegiant	52	1,817,930
jetBlue	9	1,650,210
Frontier	15	1,086,580
Spirit	9	905,410
All	**3,028**	**159,916,720**

Source: GAO analysis of DOT data.

RELATED GAO PRODUCTS

Airline Deregulation: Reregulating the Airline Industry Would Likely Reverse Consumer Benefits and Not Save Airline Pensions. GAO-06-630. Washington, D.C.: June 9, 2005.

Commercial Aviation: Bankruptcy and Pension Problems Are Symptoms of Underlying Structural Issues. GAO-05-945. Washington, D.C.: Sept. 30, 2005.

Private Pensions: The Pension Benefit Guaranty Corporation and Long-Term Budgetary Challenges. GAO-05-772T. Washington, D.C.: June 9, 2005.

Private Pensions: Government Actions Could Improve the Timeliness and Content of Form 5500 Pension Information. GAO-05-294. Washington, D.C.: June 3, 2005.

Private Pensions: Recent Experiences of Large Defined Benefit Plans Illustrate Weaknesses in Funding Rules. GAO-05-294. Washington, D.C.: May 31, 2005.

Commercial Aviation: Legacy Airlines Must Further Reduce Costs to Restore Profitability. GAO-04-836. Washington, D.C.: August 11, 2004.

Private Pensions: Publicly Available Reports Provide Useful but Limited Information on Plans' Financial Condition. GAO-04-395. Washington, D.C.: March 31, 2004.

Private Pensions: Multiemployer Plans Face Short- and Long-Term Challenges. GAO-04-423. Washington, D.C.: March 26, 2004.

Private Pensions: Timely and Accurate Information Is Needed to Identify and Track Frozen Defined Benefit Plans. GAO-04-200R. Washington, D.C.: December 17, 2003.

Pension Benefit Guaranty Corporation: Single-Employer Pension Insurance Program Faces Significant Long-Term Risks. GAO-04-90. Washington, D.C.: October 29, 2003.

Commercial Aviation: Air Service Trends at Small Communities since October 2000. GAO-02-432. Washington, D.C.: March 29, 2002.

End Notes

[1] Mergers generally refer to the combination of two companies into one company by mutual consent, while acquisitions (also called takeovers) refer to one company's purchase of assets or equity in another company on friendly or hostile terms.

[2] The seven legacy airlines (Alaska Airlines, American Airlines, Continental Airlines, Delta Air Lines, Northwest Airlines, United Airlines, and US Airways) all predated industry deregulation in 1978, while the seven low-cost airlines (AirTran Airways, America West Airlines, ATA, Frontier Airlines, JetBlue Airways, Southwest Airlines, and Spirit Airlines) entered interstate service after 1978. In 2005, America West and US Airways merged under the name US Airways.

[3] See appendix II for information on the Delta Air Lines and Northwest Airlines merger.

[4] These were the most recent data available at the time of our review.

[5] Seven legacy airlines accounted for these losses from 2001 to 2005. The four airlines filing for bankruptcy were Delta Air Lines, Northwest Airlines, United Airlines, and US Airways. In general, the legacy airlines were unprofitable at this time as a result of reduced demand following the September 11, 2001, terrorist attacks (and other external shocks), increased competition from low-cost airlines, and high cost structures.

[6] Air service markets are usually defined in terms of scheduled service between a point of origin and a point of destination. We refer to these markets as city-pair markets. The markets in our report include airlines providing both nonstop and connecting service.

[7] We defined an effective competitor as an airline with at least 5 percent of passengers within a city-pair market.

[8] Fares were inflation adjusted in 2006 dollars.

[9] Passenger traffic is measured by enplanements.

[10] The Guidelines were jointly developed by DOJ's Antitrust Division and the Federal Trade Commission (FTC) and describe the inquiry process agencies follow in analyzing proposed mergers. The most current version of the Guidelines was issued in 1992; Section 4, relating to efficiencies, was revised in 1997.

[11] Pub. L. No. 95-504, Oct. 24, 1978.

[12] Both American Eagle and American Airlines are subsidiaries of AMR Corporation.

[13] GAO, Aviation Competition: Issues Related to the Proposed United Airlines-US Airways Merger, GAO-01-212 (Washington, D.C.: Dec. 15, 2000) p. 10, footnote 6.

[14] PBGC was established under the Employee Retirement Income Security Act of 1974 (ERISA) and set forth standards and requirements that apply to defined benefit plans. PBGC was established to encourage the continuation and maintenance of voluntary private pension plans and to insure the benefits of workers and retirees in defined benefit plans should plan sponsors fail to pay benefits. PGBC operations are financed, for example, by insurance premiums paid by sponsors of defined benefit plans, investment income, assets from pension plans trusted by PBGC, and recoveries from the companies formerly responsible for the plans.

[15] The six airlines receiving loan guarantees were Aloha, World, Frontier, US Airways, ATA, and America West.

[16] Capacity is defined as available scheduled airline seats.

[17] GAO, Commercial Aviation: Bankruptcy and Pensions Problems Are Symptoms of Underlying Structural Issues, GAO-05-945 (Washington, D.C.: Sept. 30, 2005).

[18] Unless otherwise noted, all dollar amounts in this section have been adjusted to 2007 dollars.

[19] Revenue passenger miles are the number of miles paying passengers are transported and are an indicator of passenger traffic.

[20] Available seat miles are the number of seats offered by an airline multiplied by the number of scheduled miles flown. This is a typical measure of capacity in the airline industry.

[21] Cost per available seat mile (CASM) is calculated as operating expenses divided by total available seat miles. Calculating CASM allows comparisons across different sizes of airlines.

[22] See Randy Bennett, Patrick Murphy, and Jack Schmidt, "A Competitive Analysis of an Industry in Transition: The U.S. Scheduled Passenger Airline Industry." Gerchick-Murphy Associates (Washington, D.C.) July 2007.

[23] Liquidity is a measure of a firm's ability to meet short-term liabilities with cash or marketable securities.

[24] Fuel hedging allows an airline to lock in on fuel purchase prices in advance of future delivery, thus protecting against anticipated increases in the price of fuel.

[25] The airlines recently filing for bankruptcy or ceasing operations include Air Midwest, Aloha Airlines, ATA Airlines, Big Sky Air, Champion Air, EOS Airlines, Frontier Airlines, MAXjet Airways, and Skybus Airlines.

[26] The top 5,000 city-pair markets we analyzed accounted for 90 percent of all domestic passenger traffic in 2006.

[27] We defined an effective competitor to be an airline that carried at least 5 percent of passengers within a city-pair market.

[28] These figures include only passengers carried by airlines with at least 5 percent of passengers in a city-pair market; therefore an unknown number of passengers in each market were not counted.

[29] In 2006, Southwest Airlines accounted for two-thirds of the passengers carried by low-cost airlines.

[30] Because the markets that had low-cost airlines differed in 1998 and 2006, other factors that changed during that time frame, such as average distances flown, may also account for the price differences across the groupings of routes with and without low-cost competitors.

[31] These figures include only passengers carried by an airline with at least 5 percent of passengers in a city-pair market; therefore an unknown number of passengers in each market were not counted.

[32] Large hub airports are those defined in 49 U.S.C. § 40102 as commercial service airports having at least 1 percent of passenger boardings. See also 49 U.S.C. § 47102.

[33] Respondents were travel managers responsible for negotiating and managing their firms' corporate accounts.

[34] See Severin Borenstein, "Airline Mergers, Airport Dominance, and Market Power," *American Economic Review*, Vol 80, May 1990, and Steven A. Morrison, "Airline Mergers: A Longer View," *Journal of Transport Economics and Policy*, September 1996; and Gregory J. Werden, Andrew J. Joskow, and Richard L. Johnson, "The Effects of Mergers on Price and Output: Two Case Studies from the Airline Industry," *Managerial and Decision Economics*, Vol. 12, October 1991.

[35] See Steven A. Morrison, and Clifford Winston, "The Remaining Role for Government Policy in the Deregulated Airline Industry." *Deregulation of Network Industries: What's Next?* Sam Peltzman and Clifford Winston, eds. Washington, D.C., Brookings Institution Press, 2000. pp. 1-40.

[36] See Severin Borenstein, 1989, "Hubs and High Fares: Dominance and Market Power in the U.S. Airline Industry," *RAND Journal of Economics*, 20, 344-365; GAO, *Airline Deregulation: Barriers to Entry Continue to Limit Competition in Several Key Markets*, GAO/RCED-97-4 (Washington, D.C.: Oct. 18, 1996); GAO, *Airline Competition: Effects of Airline and Market Concentration and Barriers to Entry on Airfares*, GAO/RCED-91-101 (Washington, D.C.: Apr. 16, 1991).

[37] Open Skies seeks to enable greater access of U.S. airlines to Europe, including expanded rights to pick up traffic in one country in Europe and carry it to another European or third country (referred to as fifth freedom rights). Additionally, the United States will expand EU airlines' rights to carry traffic from the United States to other countries.

[38] Applications, filed in summer 2007 by SkyTeam members Air France, Alitalia, CSA Czech, Delta, KLM, and Northwest, were approved in 2008. In December 2006, DOT approved the addition of three members (Swiss International, LOT Polish, and TAP Air Portugal) to the Star Alliance's already approved immunized alliance team of Austrian, Lufthansa, German, Scandanavian, and United.

[39] Code-sharing is a marketing arrangement in which an airline places its designator code on a flight operated by another airline and sells and issues tickets for that flight.

[40] Pub. L. No. 110-161, Section 117, Dec. 26, 2007.

[41] See 15 U.S.C. § 18a(d)(1). Both DOJ and the Federal Trade Commission have antitrust enforcement authority, including reviewing proposed mergers and acquisitions. DOJ is the antitrust enforcement authority charged with reviewing proposed mergers and acquisitions in the airline industry. Additionally, under the Hart-Scott-Rodino Act, DOJ has 30 days after the initial filing to notify companies that intend to merge whether DOJ requires additional information for its review. If DOJ does not request additional information, the firms can close their deal (15 U.S.C. § 18a(b)). If more information is required, however, the initial 30-day waiting period is followed by a second 30-day period, which starts to run after both companies have provided the requested information. Companies often attempt to resolve DOJ competitive concerns, if possible, prior to the expiration of the second waiting period. Any restructuring of a transaction—e.g., through a divestiture—is included in a consent decree entered by a court, unless the competitive problem is unilaterally fixed by the parties prior to the expiration of the waiting period (called a "fix-it first").

[42] Market power is the ability to maintain prices profitably above competitive levels for a significant period of time.

[43] United States Department of Justice and Federal Trade Commission, *Horizontal Merger Guidelines* (Washington, D.C., rev. Apr. 8, 1997).

[44] More specifically, the relevant market has been defined as scheduled airline service between a point of origin and a point of destination. This is often, but not always, defined as a city-pair, but in some cases involving cities with multiple airports, the relevant market has been defined as an airport pair. In addition, DOJ has recognized that nonstop service between cities may be an important market because business travelers are less likely than leisure travelers to regard connecting service as a reasonable alternative. Thus, DOJ may see a transaction as competitively problematic because of its impact in a nonstop city-pair market.

[45] It is conceivable that a merger could also increase competition in some markets where both airlines had negligible presence before a merger, but combined the merged airlines created a stronger competitor in those markets.

[46] Remarks by J. Bruce McDonald, Deputy Assistant Attorney General, Antitrust Division, Department of Justice, presented to the Regional Airline Association President's Council Meeting, Washington, D.C., November 3, 2005.

[47] Cost savings cannot just be from a reduction in output or service.

[48] 49 U.S.C. § 41105. DOT must specifically consider the transfer of certificate authority's impact on the financial viability of the parties to the transaction and on the trade position of the United States in the international air transportation market, as well as on competition in the domestic airline industry.

[49] See Steven A. Morrison, "Actual, Adjacent, and Potential Competition: Estimating the Full Effects of Southwest Airlines," *Journal of Transport Economics and Policy*, Vol. 35, part 2, May 2001, and Austan Goolsbee and Chad Syverson, "How Do Incumbents Respond to the Threat of Entry? Evidence from the Major Airlines," *Quarterly Journal of Economics*, forthcoming.

[50] See Severin Borenstein, "U.S. Domestic Airline Pricing, 1995-2004," University of California at Berkeley, Competition Policy Center Working Papers, working paper No. CPC05-48, January 2005.

[51] Statement of John M. Nannes, Deputy Assistant Attorney General Antitrust Division, before the Committee on Judiciary, U.S. House of Representatives, Concerning Airline Hubs and Mergers, June 14, 2000.

[52] The evolution in the Guidelines' consideration of efficiencies is thoroughly explained in a paper by two former DOJ officials in 2003, see William J. Kolasky and Andrew R. Dick, "The Merger Guidelines and the Integration of Efficiencies into Antitrust Review of Horizontal Mergers," *Antitrust Law Journal* 71, 1 (2003): 207-251.

[53] See footnote 36, p. 31 of the *Horizontal Merger Guidelines* (Revised April 8, 1997).

[54] Southwest operated within the state of Texas prior to deregulation.

[55] Since 2008, ATA has filed for bankruptcy under Chapter 11 and plans to liquidate and Frontier has filed to reorganize under Chapter 11.

[56] A nonhub is a commercial service airport that has less than 0.05 percent of the passenger boardings.

CHAPTER SOURCES

The following chapters have been previously published:

Chapter 1 – This is an edited, excerpted and augmented edition of a United States Congressional Research Service publication, Report Order Code R41277, dated June 9, 2010.

Chapter 2 – This is an edited, excerpted and augmented edition of a United States Government Accountability Office publication, Report Order Code GAO-10-778T, dated May 27, 2010.

Chapter 3 – These remarks were delivered as Statement of Susan L. Kurland before the Senate Committee on Commerce, Science and Transportation, dated June 17, 2010.

Chapter 4 – These remarks were delivered as Statement of Glenn F. Tilton before the Senate Committee on Commerce, Science and Transportation, dated June 17, 2010.

Chapter 5 – These remarks were delivered as Statement of Robert Roach, Jr. before the Senate Committee on Commerce, Science and Transportation, dated June 17, 2010.

Chapter 6 – These remarks were delivered as Statement of Charles Leocha before the Senate Committee on Commerce, Science and Transportation, dated June 17, 2010.

Chapter 7 – These remarks were delivered as Statement of Daniel McKenzie before the Senate Committee on Commerce, Science and Transportation, dated June 16, 2010.

Chapter 8 – This is an edited, excerpted and augmented edition of a United States Government Accountability Office publication, Report Order Code GAO-09-393, dated April 2009.

Chapter 9 – This is an edited, excerpted and augmented edition of a United States Government Accountability Office publication, Report Order Code GAO-08-845, dated July 2008.

INDEX